AFRAID

Demon Possession and Spiritual Warfare in America

ROBERT H. BENNETT

CONCORDIA PUBLISHING HOUSE • SAINT LOUIS

Published by Concordia Publishing House
3558 S. Jefferson Ave., St. Louis, MO 63118–3968
1-800-325-3040 • www.cph.org

Scripture quotations are from the ESV Bible® (The Holy Bible, English Standard Version®), copyright © 2001 by Crossway Bibles, a publishing ministry of Good News Publishers. Used by permission. All rights reserved.

Hymn texts with the abbreviation *LSB* are from *Lutheran Service Book*, copyright © 2006 Concordia Publishing House. All rights reserved.

Quotations marked AE are from Luther's Works, American Edition (56 vols.; St. Louis: Concordia Publishing House and Philadelphia: Fortress Press, 1955–86).

Quotations marked LC are from Luther's Large Catechism in *Concordia: The Lutheran Confessions*, second edition; edited by Paul McCain et al., copyright © 2006 Concordia Publishing House. All rights reserved.

Cover art: © iStockphoto.com; dollarphotoclub.com
Image credits: © dollarphotoclub.com; iStockphoto.com; p. 58 background © Yuri Arcurs / iStockphoto.com, © Vasja Koman / iStockphoto.com; p. 76 Chris Gramly / iStockphoto.com; Shutterstock, Inc.

Manufactured in the United States of America

Library of Congress Cataloging-in-Publication Data

Bennett, Robert H.

  Afraid : demon possession and spiritual warfare in America / Robert H. Bennett.

    pages cm

  Includes bibliographical references and index.

  ISBN 978-0-7586-4939-3

  1. Spiritual warfare—United States. 2. Christianity—United States—21st century. 3. Christianity and culture—United States. 4. United States—Religion. I. Title.

  BR517.B46 2015

  239'.9--dc23   2015029467

1 2 3 4 5 6 7 8 9 10   25 24 23 22 21 20 19 18 17 16

This book is dedicated to my dear wife, Angela,
who is my constant support and helpmate.

Contents

List of Illustrations

The following photographs are copyright © Robert H. Bennett.

Key Terms

animism. From Latin *animus*, meaning "soul, life." The world-view that nonhuman entities (animals, plants, and inanimate objects or phenomena) possess a spiritual essence.

catechesis. The thorough and ongoing instruction in the basic teaching of Christian faith.

dogma. A principle or set of principles laid down by an authority as incontrovertibly true.

generational curse. A curse that is thought to be passed down from one generation to the next.

moralism. The belief that access to God can be achieved through one's personal efforts or attempts to improve oneself. Moralism, then, is nothing more than the worship of one's works.

mysticism. A practice that seeks to connect one's self to God through acts of contemplation and self-surrender.

naturalism. A philosophical viewpoint according to which everything arises from natural properties and causes, and supernatural or spiritual explanations are excluded or discounted.

necromancy. The attempt to communicate with the dead.

nihilism. The rejection of all religious and moral principles, often in the belief that life is meaningless.

paranormal. Something that is outside of normal experience or scientific explanation.

paranormal investigator. Someone who believes in numerous spiritual realities and seeks to prove their existence through pseudoscientific means.

Rationalism. The belief or theory that opinions and actions should be based on reason and knowledge rather than on religious belief or emotional response.

worldview. The lens by which someone organizes or structures the world.

ACKNOWLEDGMENTS

I wish to thank my wife, Angela, who not only constantly encouraged me while writing this book but also worked tirelessly with me on its editing. I would also like to thank my children, Robert, Joseph, Amy, and Kate, without whose support this book could not have been accomplished. Finally, I give thanks and praise to our Lord Jesus Christ, who has faithfully worked through the numerous individuals that have delivered the Holy Word and the Holy Sacraments to me, thereby connecting me to the forgiveness provided though His life, death, and resurrection. The most noteworthy of these is the sainted Rev. Dr. Ralph Fisher, who not only continually spoke the Gospel into my young ears but also instilled within me a strong desire for higher learning. To God be the praise.

INTRODUCTION

Baptism . . . now saves you, not as a removal of dirt from the body but as an appeal to God for a good conscience, through the resurrection of Jesus Christ. (1 Peter 3:21)

There are only two religions in the world. While such a statement may seem naive to the general reader, it should not sound strange to the Christian. For when the facade of this world is torn away, all that remains are two spiritual kingdoms: the kingdom of God and the kingdom of the evil one—namely, Satan. The kingdom of God is founded on Jesus, the King of kings and the Lord of lords. The kingdom of the devil is founded on a lie. His is a fallen and condemned kingdom without any hope of return to its splendor. Satan is the father of lies and is capable of becoming whatever we desire him to be. He represents himself as an angel of light (2 Corinthians 11:14) to those who will receive him as an angel; he represents himself as an ancestor to those who seek to speak to the dead; and he represents himself as a scientific principle to those who would deny God's activity in the world. Yet, in the midst of his various appearances, the strategy is always the same. It is a strategy of despair that curves an individual's focus inward into oneself, to one's works or abilities. Thus, all false religions are about the work of the individual, but the Christian religion is about the work of another: our Savior, Jesus Christ.

Afraid

The title of this book represents the general spiritual situation found in America, which also represents a common problem found worldwide. Outside the truth of Jesus' sacrificial life and death for fallen humanity, only fear can exist. Only through the revelation of Jesus can anyone understand the nature of God. Apart from divine revelation, God remains a hidden God, who seems to be unjust and unloving. He seems to be a God who acts inconsistently throughout history. Throughout time, such an understanding of God has resulted in a spirituality called animism. Animism has many varieties, but one consistent theme or understanding is that there is a creator god who may have multiple names. This god is the one who created the cosmos and all that is contained within it—either acting on his own or in connection with a lesser god. This creator god does not have a direct connection with the daily events of his creation. Does this sound familiar? It should, because animism has made a comeback in our time. One cannot turn on a television without hearing about ghosts, spirits, aliens from other planets, Bigfoot, or other strange creatures. Some may question if these things should be lumped together. Maybe you are one who does not believe in spirits or ghosts, but you do believe in Bigfoot or aliens. These last two seem more plausible to you because they do not carry with them spiritual connections. Yet, most people who believe in such things eventually find a spiritual connection with them. For instance, American Indians understand Sasquatch or Bigfoot to be a spiritual entity. Moreover, American Indian religions are becoming influential for many people who are seeking new spiritual experiences. The animistic worldview finds a spiritual reality, or essence, in many aspects of the world—seen and unseen—around them, whether plants, animals, objects, or "phenomena."

Many of those who believe in otherworldly aliens also speak of them in spiritual ways. (We will examine this more in chapter 3.) This means that the Western world as a whole, and America in particular, is moving away from a scientific approach and returning to the realm of spirituality. Animism is now in the forefront of our daily lives. To be sure, it was never really gone, but for some time it has been hidden under the surface of our culture's beliefs.[1]

The Church has begun to talk about these things again, and many pastors are surprised by what their church members are confessing to them. Stories of spirits, night terrors, and ghosts come pouring out of people's lips when they think it is safe to speak of such things. But this is a new experience for many pastors, and their lack of experience becomes problematic, especially when they give their people the impression that such things simply do not exist. Others show their unbelief by failing to address the topic of spiritual warfare. When texts referring to exorcism are included in the Gospel reading, but the topic of spiritual warfare is altogether avoided—or preached as if it was a historical event no longer to be expected in the modern day—this can cause those who are struggling with a spiritual or demonic problem to feel as though their church does not offer a safe place to speak openly about their struggles. They don't expect their pastor to believe them. However, when a pastor preaches and teaches the exorcistic texts of the Bible as an ongoing reality for the Christian, things begin to change. Longtime members of the church begin to seek the counsel of their pastors.

This leads to the next problem: most pastors, and therefore the laypeople in their communities of faith, have not been trained to deal with the topic and issues of spiritual warfare. One of the purposes of this book is to provide guidance for responding to those who have various challenges and difficulties of a spiritual nature. Most of the personal stories contained within this book are the real-life stories of people who sought pastoral help.

---

1 Peter Washington, *Madame Blavatsky's Baboon: A History of the Mystics, Mediums, and Misfits Who Brought Spiritualism to America* (New York: Shocken Books, 1993).

However, due to the personal nature of these stories, some of the details have been changed to protect the privacy and pastoral seal of Confession and Absolution.

The Church's Treasures for the Protection of the Christian

The real case studies that comprise this book demonstrate the power of Jesus' name attached to the preaching of the Word and the administration of the Sacraments. At times, the liturgical analysis will provide in-depth theological reflection on how both of these treasures of the Church become a bulwark of protection for the Christian who struggles under demonic and spiritual attack. Confession and Absolution, Holy Baptism, and the Lord's Supper in the context of Christian life and spiritual warfare become critical topics for the mission of the Church.

CONFESSION AND ABSOLUTION

Many churches provide corporate Confession and Absolution in their weekly church services, but those who face severe spiritual oppression are often unable to find specific relief in this general form of Confession and Absolution. Satan is wise and knows how to create doubt in the sinner, especially in the sinner who is plagued with despair. Indeed, we will learn that despair is one of Satan's strongest weapons, and many times it can only be wiped clean through the clear Word of God applied to the individual and his or her unique situation. Most spiritual and demonic problems can be alleviated through the simple act of individual Confession and Absolution.

HOLY BAPTISM

The importance of Holy Baptism for one who is in spiritual danger cannot be overstated. Luther informs his readers that Holy Baptism brings with it an enemy who seeks to destroy us. The enemy is the devil, and Baptism brings us into his sights and toward the top of his list. One might then ask, "Why, then, would one seek to be baptized if it brings with it such danger?" But the danger is already present. The devil prowls relentlessly in our own weak and sinful flesh and in the sinful world. Even though each of our circumstances will be different, the fact remains that all people will die, unless the Lord returns before the curse of death comes. Yet, Jesus has warned us: "Do not fear those who kill the body but cannot kill the soul. Rather fear Him who can destroy both soul and body in hell" (Matthew 10:28; cf. Luke 12:4–5). Baptism is our protection, hope, and promise. In Baptism, we are connected to Jesus' crucifixion and resurrection. The death that we face is no longer able to bring with it our eternal end. For the one who is baptized, life awaits—a much fuller life than anything experienced in this fallen world. Moreover, with Baptism comes ownership. The baptized become children of God and receive His divine name upon their foreheads. Yes, Baptism brings the rage of Satan and his demons, but it also provides the promise of protection and life.

Baptism has lifelong benefits—specifically, that we are God's children and therefore cannot be separated from His protection or promises.

HOLY COMMUNION

While Jesus' spiritual presence is promised wherever His Word is proclaimed, in His Holy Supper the Christian is connected to the bodily presence of Jesus. In the Sacrament, the child of God receives the true body and true blood of Jesus in and under the bread and the wine. It is this very body and blood given and shed upon the cross that defeated sin, death, and the devil. Holy Communion is the sustaining gift of Jesus' presence for the forgiveness of sins.

WHERE JESUS IS, SATAN MUST FLEE

Where these three gifts—Absolution, Holy Baptism, and Holy Communion—exist, Satan cannot bear to remain. In the presence of Jesus, Satan is forced to flee. Satan's release and surrender only come according to the Lord's timetable. God chooses how and when to apply the promises of His holy things. This is important to understand so that when you struggle with the devil, yet fail to receive instant relief, you don't fall into greater despair. Scripture uses the apostle Paul as an example to those who struggle with this concept. Paul describes a demonic thorn in his flesh that God refused to remove despite Paul's pleading. Although the Bible does not tell us why God did not remove this torment from the great apostle, the answer Paul receives makes it clear that God is mediating his torment. God tells Paul, "My grace is sufficient for you, for My power is made perfect in weakness" (2 Corinthians 12:9).

There is no hidden or secret truth waiting to be released to you in this book. Many Christians have been taught about the truths of these treasures of the Church from childhood, but they have simply not retained their meanings. Even those who have remembered these truths and have received great comfort from them still fall under the lies of Satan and need to hear, touch, and taste them daily as they battle their own sin, the world, and the devil.

Catechesis as Protection

During my research, it became clear that exorcism and spiritual warfare are more about catechesis than anything else. Catechesis is thorough and ongoing instruction in the basic teaching of Christian faith. In the Lutheran Church, catechetical instruction is comprised of studying the simple words of Luther's Small and Large Catechisms and the promise of Jesus that they point to in Holy Scripture. It is important for one to continually hear and pray the words of Scripture. All of us need to be reminded that we are baptized and that Baptism has lifelong benefits—specifically, that we are God's children and therefore cannot be separated from His protection or promises. All Christians need to be where the Lord has promised to be for the forgiveness of sins, and that promise is not found with any greater assurance than in the Lord's Supper. Apart from these simple things, there is no hope, because Jesus has promised to personally be in these things for us.

It is the contention of this book that Jesus is the only exorcist, and He fulfills His work through the gifts that He has promised. For those readers who do not come from a Christian sacramental background, these concepts will seem foreign and maybe even ridiculous. If you find yourself in this category, I simply ask you to continue reading and hold your doubts until you see how the promised presence of Jesus is seen in the stories this book contains.

The spirits the priest
was invoking were
not her ancestors
but instead demons
in the guise of
human spirits.

CHAPTER

1

I Am Afraid:
Asking the Devil into Your Home

Not earth nor hell's satanic crew Against us shall prevail. Their might? A joke, a mere facade! God is with us and we with God—Our vict'ry cannot fail. (*LSB* 666:3)

We begin with the story of a woman who asked the spirits into her home. She was not ready for what would come, but who could be ready for such trouble? Stories like the one provided in this chapter are increasing in frequency in the Western world, because people are more open to the occult. The occult seeks to understand the things that have not been revealed to us by God. While God's Word reveals many things that have been hidden from the foundation of the world (Matthew 13:35), sinful man always wants more. God's revealed truth is never enough.

The occult attempts to learn the secret things that God has not revealed. In this endeavor, humanity seeks answers from what it believes to be means of divination or contact with otherworldly beings. As we will learn later in this book, the naturalism of our time is leading us back into the supernatural worldview. Now, more than ever, people from Western societies are reporting ghost sightings in their homes. They are concerned about terrifying generational curses. Reports about interactions with spiritual beings are growing in American society. Indeed, this is nothing new, but in the past such beliefs were only found on the fringes of our society. However, today more and more people are living in fear of those things that go bump in the night.

The occult attempts to learn the secret things that God has not revealed.

Who among us has not awakened in the night fearful of what may surround us? Even when we tell ourselves that we don't believe in ghosts, we still remember that Satan and his demons can attack us in many ways. Many in this generation also falsely recognize that a proper veneration of the spirits sometimes provides them with material benefits. The spirits are willing to give us what we want in an attempt to redirect us from the proper focus of our dependence—namely, Jesus. Still, Satan and his demons often use fear to control people and lead them away to the deceptive spirit of the occult.

The true story you are about to read is one story among many common to our day. It demonstrates how one can be led astray from the truth and into the fear and despair that can result from seeking help from the occult. To many, the story may seem strange and unlikely, but similar stories can be found throughout American households. Many will question the prominence of such events in the American context. At one time, I, too, would have questioned such things, but I am contacted weekly by pastors who find themselves dealing with these new forms of "spirituality" springing up in their localities. Many times, even those who consider themselves to be Christians can be caught unaware of their fall into the false spirituality of our times.

Lost in the Spirituality of the Day

This story is about a young woman—a nurse—whom we will call Jill. She was unmarried and pregnant with her second child. Jill did not "come from money" and found herself struggling daily to succeed. She was a Christian, but her Christianity was formed by the preachers she followed daily on her television. Jill wondered, "What is wrong with me, and why haven't I gained the success promised to me by the television evangelists?" If she is faithful, she was told, she will prosper, but Jill had not seen any change in her circumstances since becoming a Christian.

Without a church or a pastor, Jill turned to her friends for help. One friend told her that there was a man in Miami who had the power to help her. So she called the man, and he became her spiritual advisor and protector. Jill had unknowingly connected herself with a voodoo priest from "Little Haiti" in Miami. He claimed to have the power to change her life, but his services would come at a high cost. Jill thought the cost would be only monetary, but it would be much more. . . .

Their first conversations took place over the phone. The priest prayed for her and sent her "the spirit of abundance." He told Jill that this spirit would help her to finally find success in life. When his prayers didn't seem to be helping, the voodoo priest told Jill that she had a generational curse. A generational curse is thought to be a curse that is passed down from one's ancestors. While explanations of these curses may vary, it is usually claimed that they are the result of a previous relative's particular vow made to the spirits, or a result of the vow of another person to harm the family. The curse is thought to be empowered by the spiritual world, which will only ease the curse if the one who carries it bends his or her will to that of the spirits. Whether such curses are real or hogwash, Satan and his demons take advantage of such mental doors to attack and bring despair upon their victims. The voodoo priest had Jill just where he wanted her. Without knowing it, Jill had opened herself up to the attack that was coming her way.

Upon diagnosing the problem as a generational curse, the priest told Jill that a solution would require a more personal touch. The phone calls they shared were not sufficient for such a desperate case as hers. Rather than just a simple blessing over the phone lines, he would need to come and visit her to properly remove the curse. Jill was ready to try anything, but she could never have imagined what the voodoo priest had in mind for her and her unborn child.

The arrangements were made for his visit. She would pay for his travel expenses and his services. This would not come cheap, but at this point Jill believed that whatever the cost, it would be worth it. What else could she do? She needed help, and she needed it now.

As Jill prepared to pick up the voodoo priest at the airport, she wondered what he would be like. She pictured him as her rescuer, one who would come and save her from the curse of her ancestors. Would he be young and powerful looking? She had never talked to him about such things on the phone, but Jill had expected him to be impressive.

When the voodoo priest finally emerged from the airport terminal, Jill was surprised at his age. He had sounded so young on the phone, but he had graying hair. He was well-dressed and had a striking look, making him seem to have a "hidden power" about him. The man immediately took control over the situation. He told Jill that they needed to gather the necessary supplies on the way to her home. Their first stop was the sporting goods store. As they entered the store, they walked to the very back, to the area where the firearms were sold. What did they need? The man spoke to the store clerk and was directed to one of the shelves. Gunpowder! The man explained that the ritual Jill would undergo required gunpowder. He would explain more when they got to her home. . . .

As the two of them entered Jill's house, the voodoo priest requested a few other items. He needed a piece of wood large enough for her to stand upon, pictures of Jill's deceased ancestors, and a glass of water for each of the ancestors. It was time for the ritual to begin. He told Jill to stand on the wood and then poured out the gunpowder in a circle around her. On a shelf, he placed the pictures of Jill's ancestors with a glass of water in front of each picture. He explained, "The water is your offering to the ancestors. They have the power to help you or to hurt you. By offering this sacrifice, they will be inclined to help rather than hurt." Next, the voodoo priest began calling on his spirits. To Jill, his words were unintelligible, but he was no doubt speaking in Haitian Creole. As he spoke the words of his incantation, he reached down, striking a match and igniting the gunpowder that encircled her. Dark smoke filled Jill's nose as the voodoo priest continued to chant over her. Following the ritual, Jill was instructed to put the wooden board in a safe place within the home and to keep her children from ever touching it.

Next, the voodoo priest reached into his bag and removed a bar of dark black soap. Voodoo priests use black soap as one of the ingredients in what they call "African Money Spell." The soap can cost as much as $250 per bar, but it promises to bring much money to the one who uses it properly in the bathing ritual. The priest instructed Jill to bathe with the soap on the morning of each full moon and recite the words provided to her. He told her that the curse laid upon her was a difficult one and that there was still even more that she must undergo to properly remove the curse.

The final ritual that Jill was required to undergo was the most disturbing. The voodoo priest asked Jill to expose her pregnant belly to him. After Jill removed her shirt, the man started rubbing a dark voodoo potion upon her belly. While his hands moved over the thin flesh covering the baby in her womb, the priest began to chant the voodoo spell upon her unborn child. Looking back on the event, Jill admitted that she was disgusted with herself for allowing this stranger such access to her child. The man told her that the ritual was necessary to protect the child from the spirits. He explained to the mother-to-be that when he cast the spirits from her, they would seek to enter the closest person to her, in this case the child within her womb. Jill was placing herself and her child directly into the hands of a false prophet. The spirits the priest was invoking were not her ancestors but instead demons in the guise of human spirits.

The spirits the priest was invoking were not her ancestors but instead demons in the guise of human spirits.

With this last ritual completed, the voodoo priest required his price. Jill did not reveal the amount of money she was required to pay the priest, but she was clear that it was a substantial amount, more than she could pay at the time. After some negotiations, Jill and the voodoo priest agreed on the terms of his payment. Knowing that she might decide to hold back his payment after his departure, the voodoo priest warned Jill about the consequences she would face if she did not repay her debt to him. Jill remembers him saying, "If you fail to pay even one payment, the spirits will return with even more terrifying spirits to destroy your life and the lives of your children."

The man whom Jill had hoped would reassure her that morning now overwhelmed her with fear and disgust. She held back her disdain as she drove him to the airport. For the first few months, Jill sent him the payments as they had agreed. In those months, Jill did not notice any improvement in her condition. In fact, she was even more afraid than she had been in the past. After some time had passed, she finally decided to reach out to a Christian pastor for help. Jill was embarrassed by her actions, but she knew she needed help. The pastor admitted that he had never heard of such things, but he suggested that she should break all contact with the man. After some thought, Jill decided that she would follow the pastor's advice. The voodoo priest was furious that she had not sent her required payments and threatened her with what was soon to come her way. The spirits would be back but this time with a vengeance.

From Where Does My Help Come?

From the time Jill cut off her connection to the voodoo priest she was under constant spiritual attack. Jill saw visions of dead relatives, dark shadow people, and a few times she was even physically attacked. Moreover, her youngest child, the one who had undergone the voodoo ritual while still in his mother's womb, also experienced similar visions and terrifying nightmares. Jill needed help, and she needed it right away.

Jill rarely attended church, but she happened to work with a chaplain from the Lutheran Church. One day, in passing, she asked the chaplain if he had any experience with the things she was continuing to face. He had done a number of house blessings (another name for a home exorcism) and told her he would come to her home and pray with her.

Within a few days, the pastor met Jill at her home. He spoke to her about Jesus and His protection for those who trusted in Him. The home was a small but well-kept two bedroom duplex. The pastor went from room to room speaking the words of dedication and exorcism. He concluded the dedication by singing the hymn "A Mighty Fortress Is Our God." At first, things seemed to improve, but the strange occurrences did not completely go away. The pastor told Jill that Jesus is the one who protects His people and that she should continue the prayers in her home. He also told her that he would return if she thought she needed him. It was not long before she made another request for him to visit. This time, the pastor sought the help of another pastor who had more experience with the demonic. The date was set: the two pastors would visit and speak the words of Jesus upon Jill and her home.

As the pastors entered Jill's home, they were warmly greeted. The lights were turned low in the house and the television was on as they sat down to talk. The pastors listened as Jill told them her story, then they proceeded to perform another house blessing.

How does one go about doing a home blessing? To put the answer into its proper context, one must first consider the amount of time the pastors spent at the house. In this case, it was about two and a half hours. While the exorcism only took about twenty minutes, it was necessary before the exorcism to learn more about Jill and her experiences. She was in need of pastoral assistance. Jill first needed to learn who she was in Jesus if she was going to be able to deal with the spirits that were causing her harm. Although she had been baptized as a young girl, she had never been taught the significance of her Baptism. Jill needed catechizing; she needed to be taught the Christian faith, specifically what her Baptism meant and the promises it contains.

What do Christians need to know as they face the author of sin—the devil—and his demons? Dr. Martin Luther provides some of the most helpful advice for all Christians:

> Lo, when I believe this with my whole heart, then I have the greatest treasure, namely, the death of Christ and the power which it has wrought, and I am more concerned with that than with what I have done. Therefore, devil, begone with both my righteousness and my sin. If I have committed some sin, go eat the dung; it's yours. I'm not worrying about it, for Jesus Christ died. St. Paul bids me comfort myself with this, that I may learn to defend myself from the devil and say: Even though I have sinned, it doesn't matter; I will not argue with you about what evil or good I have done. There is no time to talk of that now; go away and do it some other time when I have been a bad boy, or go to the impenitent and scare them all you please. But with me, who have already been through the anguish and throes of death, you'll find no place now. This is not the time for arguing, but for comforting myself with the words that Jesus Christ died and rose for me. Thus I am sure that God will bring me, along with other Christians, with Christ to his right hand and carry me through death and hell.[2]

While Luther's words may seem a bit crude to some, they are blunt and to the point. Luther knew that the prideful devil could not bear to be belittled nor to have his pride attacked. Luther's response would make for good memory work for all Christians. Our righteousness is never found in our works or actions, for such will always be tainted with the sin that clings to us. No, our righteousness is found only in Jesus, who died and carried our sins to a cross. Nothing is left to do. Even repentance is a gift of God to

---

2   AE 51:241–42.

His baptized children (Luke 24:46–47; Acts 5:31–32; 2 Corinthians 7:10; 2 Timothy 2:25; Hebrews 6:1). This was the lesson Jill needed to learn.

Jill had not properly understood the Gospel. She needed to understand who she was in Christ Jesus. In talking with Jill, it became clear to the pastors that her conscience was plagued with the sins she had committed against God. Jill thought herself to be lost and without hope because she had brought the voodoo priest into her family's life. She believed that she was under a generational curse, and as a result of that curse neither she nor her children would ever prosper. This lie was perpetuated through the false claims of the "prosperity gospel," which had added to her despair.

The devil is a liar and his followers continue in his ways. Jill had committed many serious sins by attaching herself to the voodoo priest and ultimately to Satan, whom he served. Because of the lie she was holding on to, Jill was trapped in a life of despair. She did not understand the promise of Jesus' Gospel for her. She needed to hear the gracious, life-giving Gospel that had claimed her as a child of God when she was baptized into His name, with all the promises of forgiveness, life, and the resurrection. What of her sins? Once again, Luther's response is the right response whenever we are attacked by Satan and his demons' condemning words: "Even though I have sinned, it doesn't matter; I will not argue with you about what evil or good I have done. There is no time to talk of that now; go away."[3] Luther speaks in the realm of exorcism. The word *exorcism* simply means "depart," or as Luther put it, "go away." Depart in the name of Jesus! Christ Jesus died for my sin, and there is nothing left for you, devil, to claim against me. These are words of absolution. When sins are absolved, the doubt and despair attached to them are cast off. The accusations of the devil are put to rest, and he is cast away. In this sense, I maintain that Absolution is a form of exorcism.

Jill, who had experienced such terror in her home, had asked the pastors to exorcise her house. But what she really needed was to confess her sins and hear the forgiveness that comes in Absolution. That is where

3   AE 51:241.

the pastors began. Jill confessed her unfaithfulness, which included her problematic background and a host of other sins that tormented her. The response Jill heard was strong and to the point: "In the stead and by the command of my Lord Jesus Christ I forgive you all your sins in the name of the Father and of the Son and of the Holy Spirit."

Confession and Absolution is lost to many in the Christian Church today. Roman Catholics continue a form of private Confession and Absolution, but the practice, called penance, has some shortcomings. Only the specific sins that are confessed receive the absolution and then only when the required penance (a requirement assigned by the priest) is completed. Such a system can leave doubt in the sinner's mind as to the validity of the absolution. The question arises, "Did I do everything that was required of me to complete the process?" "What sins did I hold back or forget to confess before the priest?" "Did I properly complete my required penance?" Satan is always working through our doubts. He will exploit any weakness.

For those who adhere to American Evangelicalism or the Reformed tradition, confession and absolution is something that takes place between the sinner and God. In this form, the confession is not heard by another person; therefore, in turn, the person offering the confession does not hear any words of absolution. He or she may read the promises from the Gospel (1 John 1:9), which are true promises, but Satan and his demons are masters at causing people to question if such forgiveness can cover the sins they have committed.

The Lutheran form of confession is distinctly different from the Roman Catholic and the Evangelical or Reformed practices of confession and absolution. For Lutherans, the purpose of confession is to hear absolution. The repentant person confesses his sin (specific or general) to a pastor and then hears that his sins are forgiven from the pastor (John 20:21–23)—the one who is a called representative of God. The Lutheran Rite of Confession and Absolution empties the devil's arsenal of tricks by taking all of the requirements of Absolution away from the person hearing the Words of Absolution and placing them into the hands of the Savior. "You are forgiven; go in peace." This is the absolution that Jill needed to hear. It is an absolution we all need to hear, on a continuous basis, if we are to overcome the fiery arrows of the devil and his demons (Ephesians 6:16).

Following her confession and absolution, Jill had many questions about the things she had experienced. What about angels? Jill had reported seeing them. What about ghosts? She had reported seeing them also. What about curses? Jill had thought herself to be under one. These and many other questions were asked and answered. If you have similar questions, you will find the answers as you continue to read through the stories in this book. Most important, you need to recognize what Jill needed to recognize—specifically, that Satan and his demons cannot be trusted. Their arguments and accusations seem indisputable, but hidden behind the "truth" of their words are only lies (John 8:44).

Jill had been constantly terrorized in her home. Yet, she was a child of God who had received the promise of Jesus in her Baptism, that He would never leave her nor forsake her. Jesus' words are clear, "Behold, I am with you always, to the end of the age" (Matthew 28:20). Jesus had promised to be with Jill on the day of her Baptism, but she had not understood this truth. All that Jill could think about was the terror found in her home and the curse that she believed she and her children carried.

What were the terrors that Jill had been undergoing? She had on numerous occasions noticed a dark shadowy figure lurking around her house. Flames had come out of nowhere from the stove top to burn her hands. The voodoo priest had constantly tormented her in her dreams. He would stand before her each night and remind her that he would continue to torment her for not paying her debt. Things in the house would move around on their own. Moreover, she would find white chicken feathers (chicken sacrifices are common in voodoo rituals) throughout her home, but she had no feathers or down pillows. These and many other things had caused her difficulty for more than ten years. Moreover, Jill's child, who had been part of the voodoo ritual while still in the womb, continued to have nightmares depicting his mother as a monster who was trying to kill him. He would get up at night and see Jill sitting in the front room of the house with dirty clothing and a horrible look upon her face. But when he would return to his room, he would see his mother fast asleep in her bed.

Such stories seem too fanciful for modern thinkers to comprehend. The "enlightened world" has no room for the supernatural, but spiritualism is returning, and such beliefs are becoming more common in our society. Still, for the Christian, such beliefs are not fanciful. Jesus came to destroy the works of the devil (1 John 3:8). If the Christian were to deny the works of the devil, they would be denying Scripture. The apostle Peter is clear: the devil continually seeks to cause harm to God's creation (1 Peter 5:8). Moreover, St. Paul reminds us that even after Jesus' crucifixion, death, resurrection, and ascension, we continue to live in a spiritual battlefield (Ephesians 6:12). For Jill, the battlefield had entered her home.

Prayer is an important aspect of the Christian life, and although Jill knew that she needed to pray, she had the wrong understanding of prayer. She had viewed prayer as an incantation. She was not praying to her Lord, who could deliver her from the spirits that tormented her. Instead, she had been directing her prayers to the spirits. Jill viewed prayer as magic. If she was fearful or had any paranormal experiences, she would begin praying the Lord's Prayer. She did so thinking that it was her action of reciting the prayer that would bring her comfort and protection, but prayer is not to be used as a charm, spell, or talisman. Christian prayer seeks help from Jesus. Prayer is a conversation with God, who has promised to be with us and never forsake us.

Prayer that is used as an incantation becomes idolatry and is against the First Commandment, which prohibits us from having other gods. What does it mean to have other gods? Luther is helpful here as well:

> You shall have Me alone as your God. What is the meaning of this, and how is it to be understood? What does it mean to

have a god? Or, what is God? Answer: A god means that from which we are to expect all good and in which we are to take refuge in all distress. So, to have a God is nothing other than trusting and believing Him with the heart. I have often said that the confidence and faith of the heart alone make both God and an idol. (LC I 1–3)

Even prayer can become a false god when we use it in any way not intended by God. When people use prayer as a charm, spell, talisman, or an incantation, they are attempting to use it to make something magical happen. Such is the way that the animistic peoples of the traditional religions would treat prayer. Instead, prayer is meant to be used as a conversation with the One who has all power to do all things—namely, Christ Jesus.

If you are struggling with this concept, it could be that you, too, have been using prayer as more of a false idol rather than the way true prayer is offered. Many times, things that appear to be "Christian" in effect are not. Many of the prayers and rituals of the various false religions, including voodoo, can appear to be Christian, but in fact they seek to manipulate either God or the lesser spirits, which is idolatry. In Jill's case, she recognized that she was not seeking the protection of Jesus but was speaking the words of her "prayer" to defend against the evil that was attacking her.

Many times, things that appear to be "Christian" in effect are not.

Finally, after over two hours of conversation, the pastors began the blessing of the home (an exorcism of place). They started the ritual with a hymn from the *Lutheran Service Book*, "O Little Flock, Fear Not the Foe" (*LSB* 666). This hymn mocks Satan as a defeated foe before Jesus: "Not earth nor hell's satanic crew Against us shall prevail. Their might? A joke, a mere facade!" (st. 3).

The placement of this hymn in the *Lutheran Service Book* as hymn number 666 was not accidental. It is perfectly placed within the hymnal and easily found by anyone who seeks it. Yet, it is not alone in the hymnal.

The *Lutheran Service Book* has more than seventy hymns that are exorcistic in nature. By calling these hymns "exorcistic," I mean that they directly oppose Satan and/or his evil angels. You will find a list of these helpful exorcistic hymns in the appendix at the back of the book.

Any of the hymns listed in the table could have been chosen as a way to begin the house blessing, but the hymn "O Little Flock, Fear Not the Foe" spoke specifically to Jill's spiritual condition of fear. After they sang this hymn, one of the pastors explained its meaning to Jill stanza by stanza. A short summary is provided:

> Stanza 1: O little flock, fear not the foe
> Who madly seeks your overthrow;
> > Dread not his rage and pow'r.
> And though your courage sometimes faints,
> His seeming triumph o'er God's saints
> > Lasts but a little hour.

The devil is a powerful foe in comparison to we who are fallen human beings. This stanza recognizes that the devil is real and that he seeks to overthrow our faith and hope in Jesus and cast us into despair. In this stanza, we recognize that our "courage sometimes faints." Looking in from the outside, it appears that Satan is winning this battle both within us and in the world in which we live. These words directly described Jill as she was being terrified by Satan's demons nightly in her home. With the recognition of Satan's power and might, the stanza prepares its readers for the comfort that comes in Jesus.

> Stanza 2: Be of good cheer; your cause belongs
> To Him who can avenge your wrongs;
> > Leave it to Him, our Lord.
> Though hidden yet from mortal eyes,
> His Gideon shall for you arise,
> > Uphold you and His Word.

In spite of the recognition of the powerful adversary who is seeking to destroy us, God's saints, we can be of good cheer. Jesus has the power to avenge the evil done to us. While we are many times incapable of seeing the spiritual battle that is taking place around us, this stanza assures us that even if these things are hidden from our eyes, God has provided His holy angels to fight on our behalf.

God has provided His holy angels to fight on our behalf.

By this time, Jill had recognized that she was powerless against the spirits who were molesting her. Even if Jill could not see them, God's holy angels were there protecting her. These words brought great comfort to her. After all the years of trying to face these spirits on her own, Jill finally recognized that she was powerless on her own. But she wasn't on her own: now she knew that God was with her.

Stanza 3 reaffirms that these promises are true and that for the children of God only victory awaits.

> Stanza 3: As true as God's own Word is true,
> Not earth nor hell's satanic crew
>   Against us shall prevail.
> Their might? A joke, a mere facade!
> God is with us and we with God—
>   Our vict'ry cannot fail.

God's Word is true! While stanza 1 recognizes that Satan is a powerful foe seeking to overthrow us, this stanza speaks of Satan and his demons as they stand before the stronger man, Jesus. A reminder from the Epistle to the Colossians will serve to be helpful at this point:

> [Jesus] is the image of the invisible God, the firstborn of all creation. For by Him all things were created, in heaven and on earth, visible and invisible, whether thrones or dominions or rulers or authorities—all things were created through Him and for Him. And He is before all things, and in Him all things hold together. And he is the head of the body, the church. He is the beginning, the firstborn from the dead, that in every-

thing He might be preeminent. For in Him all the fullness of God was pleased to dwell, and through Him to reconcile to Himself all things, whether on earth or in heaven, making peace by the blood of His cross. (Colossians 1:15–20)

Satan and his demons are created beings. Jesus is the creator of all things, and in Him everything and everyone finds their origin. Creation can only continue because Jesus holds it together. Satan is weak and feeble in contrast to Jesus. John's Gospel reminds us that Jesus removed Satan from his throne through His crucifixion. John records Jesus' words, "Now is the judgment of this world; now will the ruler of this world be cast out. And I, when I am lifted up from the earth, will draw all people to myself" (John 12:31–32). The phrase "cast out" comes from the Greek word *ek-ballō*,[4] which is translated into English as "exorcize." Jesus' crucifixion is the deciding act that exorcizes Satan from his position of power, thereby rendering Satan and his demons powerless. The power Satan wields is "a joke, a mere facade!" The act of the crucifixion has insured that our "vict'ry cannot fail."

> Stanza 4: Amen, Lord Jesus, grant our prayer;
> Great Captain, now Thine arm make bare,
>> Fight for us once again!
> So shall Thy saints and martyrs raise
> A mighty chorus to Thy praise
>> Forevermore. Amen.

Here, we see the object of our prayers: Jesus. He is the "Great Captain," and our prayer to Him is that He would "fight for us once again!" Jill no longer needed to fight a battle against the spirits within her home. Jesus would be the focus of her prayers as she took her place next to the mighty chorus of all of those who had gone before her in faith toward the victory that is ensured through Jesus.

---

4 For more on this, see Robert H. Bennett, *I Am Not Afraid: Demon Possession and Spiritual Warfare: True Accounts from the Lutheran Church of Madagascar* (St. Louis: Concordia, 2013), 101–4, 126–28.

Jill broke out in a smile. She said, "It all makes sense now. Jesus is with me, so I don't have to be afraid." The promise of Jesus had turned Jill's fear into strength. Like so many others whom you will read about in the coming chapters, Jill had been living in fear. But the promise of Jesus brings freedom from fear. After Confession and Absolution and catechesis, Jill was ready for the exorcism of her home to continue.

The pastors began in the bedroom, proceeded from room to room, and completed the exorcism in the living room. In each room, they read a number of Scripture passages and commanded Satan and his demons to depart in the name of Jesus. One need not use prescribed scriptural passages, but in this case they read John 14:12–17; Mark 16:15–20; Matthew 18:18–20; John 20:21–23; and concluded with John 12:31–37. The significance of each of these texts will be described later in this book.

Beggars before a Faithful God

After reading the various texts and preaching a short sermon on each one, the exorcism concluded with "A Mighty Fortress Is Our God," another exorcistic hymn found in the *Lutheran Service Book* (656 and 657):

> A mighty fortress is our God,
>   A trusty shield and weapon;
> He helps us free from ev'ry need
>   That hath us now o'ertaken.
> The old evil foe
> Now means deadly woe;
>   Deep guile and great might
>   Are his dread arms in fight;
> On earth is not his equal.
>
> With might of ours can naught be done,
>   Soon were our loss effected;
> But for us fights the valiant One,
>   Whom God Himself elected.
> Ask ye, Who is this?

Jesus Christ it is,
  Of Sabaoth Lord,
  And there's none other God;
He holds the field forever.

Though devils all the world should fill,
  All eager to devour us,
We tremble not, we fear no ill;
  They shall not overpow'r us.
This world's prince may still
Scowl fierce as he will,
  He can harm us none.
  He's judged; the deed is done;
One little word can fell him.

The Word they still shall let remain
  Nor any thanks have for it;
He's by our side upon the plain
  With His good gifts and Spirit.
And take they our life,
Goods, fame, child, and wife,
  Though these all be gone,
  Our vict'ry has been won;
The Kingdom ours remaineth.

The themes from the hymns "A Mighty Fortress Is Our God" and "O Little Flock, Fear Not the Foe" are similar. Here, once again, Christians are reminded that they have no power when faced with the evil of Satan and his demons. While this is true, the hymn points to One who is a "mighty fortress" protecting us from the "deadly foe," who seeks to bring us to "deadly woe." Who can stand against Satan and his power? No one in this world has even a chance because "on earth is not his equal." In fact, "With might of ours can naught be done, Soon were our loss effected." Too often people forget this warning. The danger of terror, despair, and even the possibility of suicide follow from failing to recognize this warning. As a result of the fall into sin, we are damaged goods. While the focus of this book puts a heavy emphasis on the activities of the devil and his demons, it is necessary to recognize that the spiritual battle we face is only enhanced by the devil's activities.

Luther reminds us in the explanation of the Sixth Petition of the Lord's Prayer that due to original sin, everyone faces a three-front battle. Our battle is against the devil, the world, and our sinful nature. This means that not all temptations are due to the devil directly, but the world and the flesh mediate most temptations. Satan is always the original source of these temptations but not the immediate source. As a result, we have no hope in fighting a spiritual battle on our own. Yet, people continue to seek spirituality apart from the Church. The Church is the place where Jesus has promised to be for our protection, forgiveness, and life. It is to Jesus that the hymn now turns, "But for us fights the valiant One . . . Jesus Christ it is, Of Sabaoth Lord, And there's none other God; He holds the field forever." Jesus is the only hope for a fallen world that seeks to destroy itself. Moreover, he is the Lord of Sabaoth. The word *Sabaoth* means "armies"—that is, the heavenly host, the holy warrior angels of heaven. In Scripture, we learn that one-third of the angels followed Satan in his rebellion (Revelation 12:3–9). Moreover, Scripture is clear that the evil angels no longer carry the power of God. The only strength the fallen angels continue to possess is that which they received at creation. While the thought of such powerful beings is sure to cause anyone fear, it should not. Scripture is also clear that holy angels who remained faithful to God (two-thirds of an unnumbered army [Hebrews 12:22]), retain the power to act in God's stead. They do so at the command of Jesus, who "holds the field forever." Therefore, when we are in Jesus, the devil and his followers have no power over us. The words of the hymn are clear: Satan and his evil angels are judged in Jesus' crucifixion. The devil "can harm us none. He's judged; the deed is done; One little word can fell him." While many have provided possible answers as to the "one word" that can stop the devil, the only proper answer is Jesus. He is the One who holds all things together and provides for all that we have in this life and the next (Colossians 1:15–20).

It is true that we must continue to live in this world of pain, but the final stanza of Luther's hymn brings our situation into perspective. There is nothing that can be taken away from us that is not a gift from God. The devil and the world can seek to destroy all that we have, "our life, goods, fame, child, and wife," but just as God has provided them for us, He is the same One who can replace them in the new creation.

Therefore, "Though these all be gone, Our vict'ry has been won; The Kingdom ours remaineth." This is the victory that belonged to Jill, who had sat in terror for more than ten years. Could Jill be freed from the attacks of Satan and his evil angels? No, none of us still living have received that promise, as we still contend against the "old evil foe." But we are promised that we are connected to Jesus' crucifixion and resurrection through the gift of Baptism (Romans 6:4–11). Death has been defeated, and we have the victory in Jesus. In the end, this is the only thing that matters, and it is the only promise that can sustain us in our final hours of life. When death draws near, Satan is sure to come calling. Luther reminds us that we are all only beggars, but we have a faithful God who will not fail us. These are the things Jill learned that day. She learned the significance of this hymn before she and the pastors sang it together. As Jill sang, her voice was strong. She sang with the promise of victory in her Lord Jesus Christ.

What will happen to Jill? Will these spirits leave her in peace? Maybe, maybe not, but she is in peace no matter what the spirits do in the end. She is connected to Jesus, who is her only true peace, "A trusty shield and weapon." As you proceed through this book, you will see that Jill's story is not as exclusive as you may have thought.

Chapter 1 Study Questions

1. How does Confession and Absolution come into play in the midst of spiritual warfare? Explain your answer using examples from the chapter.

2. What role can proper catechesis play in the midst of spiritual warfare? Explain your answer using examples from the chapter.

3. What example does Martin Luther provide when dealing with demonic assault?

4. What does "prosperity preaching" teach? How did the prosperity preaching that Jill encountered help lead her into the spiritual darkness she endured?

5. Describe Jill's view of prayer. How could this view of prayer be problematic?

6. How can the promise of Holy Baptism help us with the spiritual battles we face?

7. How can Christian hymns provide assistance to those who are spiritually oppressed or possessed?

8. Review the list of hymns provided in the appendix. How can these hymns be described as exorcistic in nature?

9. Are you aware of any exorcistic hymns that are not included in the appendix but that might be helpful to one who is spiritually oppressed or possessed? If so, what are they, and where can they be found?

10. Describe the problems of attempting to engage in a spiritual battle by oneself.

Many times, things that appear to be "Christian" in effect are not.

CHAPTER

2

Voodoo and American Spirituality

*It is shameful even to speak of the things that they do in secret.
(Ephesians 5:12)*

If you want to get a glimpse of the spiritualism that is permeating the rest of the country, New Orleans's French Quarter is a good place to start. Public nudity, drug and alcohol abuse, vampire subculture, and prostitution are the norm in the French Quarter. What is typically hidden deep in the dark corners of American society is far from hidden in this city. But there is more going on there than just moral decay. I had never been to New Orleans before writing this book, but I knew a trip was necessary if I was going to do so.

The Occult in America—A Morning Walk through the Streets of the French Quarter

New Orleans can be a beautiful city in the morning: flowers in bloom, the peacefulness of the Riverwalk, and the taste of beignets and coffee make for a beautiful beginning to any day. The streets are empty as the stench of the vomit is washed away by the street cleaners. The humidity is already weighing heavily upon anyone who is still able to walk about the streets.

But the French Quarter is as much a location of the occult as it is a place to party. Already by eight o'clock in the morning, the diviners are ready to advise the lost. The Voodoo Bones Lady has a large table open for business at the entrance of St. Louis Cathedral. For those who have not visited, this may seem difficult to believe, but this is the place to get your fortune read in the French Quarter. Yes, even in the early morning hours, you can find the diviners and fortune-tellers sitting at their card tables lined up in a row directly in front of the entrance to the cathedral. If you have visited the cathedral's courtyard, you know what I am talking about. Whatever time of day or night you choose, these spiritual practitioners' tables are awaiting you. To be sure, the tables are more active in the evenings, but to see such activity, and so early in the morning, simply caught me off guard. Yet, this was just the beginning. New Orleans is also known for its famous voodoo shops. One of the most famous carries the name of the city's most notable voodoo queen: Marie Laveau.

A Child Adds to His Voodoo Collection

Marie Laveau's story can be found in books and songs. One of the most popular songs about her was written in 1974 by Shel Silverstein and performed famously by Bobby Bare, titled simply "Marie Laveau." An Internet search will provide hours of reading about the First Woman of New Orleans voodoo, but we don't need to concern ourselves with her history.

Entering through the doors of Marie Laveau's House of Voodoo doesn't seem nearly as exotic as one might think. It is similar to other stores that crowd the French Quarter. The first things that anyone entering the store would notice are sure to be the pictures of the Catholic saints plastered on the walls. Surrounding the pictures are shelves of do-it-yourself spell bags, all lined up in alphabetical order. The place was interesting enough, but when I stopped in during my morning walk, I was not there to look at the voodoo supplies. I had spent the past few years interviewing the voodoo priests of Haiti while researching for a different book. No, I was there to people watch. What type of people come into this kind of place? You might be surprised.

Not long after I entered the store, I saw a well-dressed father along with his early teenage son coming through the doors. They were all smiles as they entered, and it soon became obvious that this was not their first visit to the store. As they entered, the father pointed to a poster of Marie Laveau and asked his son, "What about this?" The poster depicted a scantily clad Marie Laveau wrapped up by a snake, which was a depiction of the voodoo god Damballa. The man's son, seemingly annoyed at his father's suggestion, said, "No, Dad, I don't have room for that on the voodoo wall of my room." Yes, that's right; the young boy had a voodoo wall in his room and was being encouraged by his father to add to its collection. The boy then proceeded to go over to some smaller prints on the far wall and chose a copy of Laveau's death certificate. Showing the death certificate to his father, he said, "I'll take this one." He went on to explain to his father about various voodoo rites. The two of them then walked around the store a bit more. The boy was not done shopping. He looked through the do-it-yourself spell bags and handed his father a number of them along with other esoteric items. Without a word, the father reached into his back pocket to pull out his wallet and proceeded to pay for the items. The two of them happily departed the store ready to add to the boy's voodoo collection.

How Do I Get Rid of This Curse?

I visited a number of other voodoo shops on that morning walk. But after seeing one or two of the French Quarter's voodoo shops, you have seen them all. So why bother wasting the morning with another one? It is all about the people; sometimes it is just about observing the customers with their requests and questions, and at other times it's just their outward reactions, but you can learn something about American spirituality from every one of them.

Yet it is not only the customers that are worth observing. In one particular shop, the owner also had my interest. He was a tall man, with long, dark, witchlike hair, wearing a white T-shirt and blue jeans. Moments after I entered the larger-than-normal shop, his phone rang. As I listened in on the conversation, it became obvious that the person on the line felt he had a curse and was calling the shopkeeper, a voodoo practitioner, for help. While I am not able to recount all of the conversation, most of what I heard was informative as he offered his advice to the nervous caller. The voodoo priest told the caller that he did not have his tarot cards with him, so he could only guess about the spirit that had attached himself to the caller. He told the caller, "It doesn't matter which spirit is causing you the trouble through this curse. The spell that I will give you should remove just about any spiritual problem."

This was the spell suggested to the caller: "First, you must get a gallon of water. Then take the water to any priest or pastor and ask them to pray over the water. Don't worry about what they pray for. Their words don't matter. The thing that matters is that they pray. After they pray over the water, it is necessary that you pay them for their services. If you don't pay them, the spell will not work."

The voodoo priest told the man to then add the "holy water" to whatever he liked to drink. It could be tea or lemonade. He was clear that whatever the caller desired to add the water to was fine. He could even drink it plain if he wanted. The priest then told the caller to recite the words of Psalm 23 seven times, taking a drink of the water after every recitation. This procedure was to be followed seven times "because seven is God's number, and He is the creator of all things who is stronger than the one who torments you." The priest then explained to the caller that if he had a curse or a spirit attached to him, "He will feel unnaturally bloated."

After reciting the words to Psalm 23 seven times and drinking the water seven times, the caller was then instructed: "Now add sea salt and sage to the last glass of water. Both of these have the power to overcome the evil spirits. The salt must be sea salt, because other salts will not work. The sea is the place of the siren (mermaid), and the siren is the most powerful of spirits. The sage has the ability to remove all spirits from your location. Add these two things to the water and recite the words to Psalm 23 an eighth time. This last cup of enhanced water stands for the eighth day, which is the day of healing. Now after this, you will be healed, because God can heal all things." At this point, the voodoo priest entered a small room off to the side of the store, preventing me from overhearing the end of the conversation.

What I found most interesting about the conversation was the casual way it progressed. For the voodoo priest, this was obviously a common occurrence. Although I was unable to hear the conversation from the caller's perspective, there was no indication from the voodoo priest that the caller thought his advice to be out of the ordinary. This was a typical day in the life of these voodoo practitioners. That is the point: the stories in this book present real people who are afraid of the problems of life and are seeking spiritual answers apart from the Church. They are typical American citizens, not foreigners, not newly nationalized citizens. They are truly expressing an American spirituality.

A Trip to the Voodoo Temple

As I went on to investigate various sites in the area, one place continued to come up in my research: a voodoo temple. The temple stands apart from the numerous voodoo shops spread about the French Quarter, but it is still within walking distance from most of the French Quarter hotels. While most of the voodoo shops I visited had a touch of tourism attached to them, this place seemed to be the most authentic, reminding me of the voodoo temples I had visited in the backcountry of Haiti. At first glance, the shop did not give away its secrets. It seemed somewhat unimpressive. The other shops in town seemed to go out of their way to impress the customer with their "authenticity," but this shop was missing the touristy gifts and spell bags one normally could find. To be sure, there were a few things for sale but in seemingly limited quantities. I must admit that I was unimpressed and somewhat disappointed that I had made the walk all the way from my hotel just to see this empty little place. I remember thinking to myself, "At least the cemeteries are only a short walk from here." Even though the place was unimpressive, since I had made the trip to this obscure location I thought I might as well look around.

I wondered, "What was all the hype about?" The Internet search I had done revealed this place to be one of the few "authentic" voodoo locations open to the public—but then again, nearly every voodoo shop in the French Quarter of New Orleans claims the same thing. As a result, I thought it strange to see far fewer customers than I had seen in the other shops.

The most important thing to do when investigating such places is to look for the unimpressive. What is the shop telling you in its quiet ways? As I approached the rear of the shop, I noticed that affixed to the threshold was a small sign produced on a home printer. It read, "Do not enter the temple without permission." As I read the sign, I overheard a young couple speaking to the voodoo priestess, "May we enter the temple and place our offering?" The priestess told them they may but added, "You must place your gift into the hands of the idol for the blessing to work." The young couple then walked to the back of the store where I had noticed the sign. They were clearly in love. If I had to guess their ages, I would say they were in their early- to mid-twenties. Both of them were smiling and holding hands as they moved to the back of the store. After looking around a bit more, I finally built up the courage to request permission to enter the temple. "May I go in the back to look around?" The priestess responded with a chuckle in her voice and asked, "Are you sure you want to go in the back?" Chuckling again and without waiting for my answer, she replied, "Okay, go ahead." The entire time, she was smiling with an inquisitive expression on her face.

There was something different about the woman that I had not recognized in the other voodoo priest. She reminded me of the voodoo practitioners I had met in Haiti. In Haiti, it was very clear who the authentic voodoo priests were and which ones were just putting on a show. The real voodoo priests have a certain confidence about them. They are not there to scare you or even to try to impress you. Moreover, they don't hide their secrets or their power. When interviewed, they are very upfront with their answers. This woman was just like them. For a moment, it seemed that I had left the United States and traveled to the central region of Haiti. As it turned out, I was not too far off base. While not from Haiti, she was from the birthplace of Haitian voodooism; she had come to the United States directly from the African country of Benin, the birthplace of traditional voodoo. Many Haitian voodoo practitioners who have the resources travel to Benin seeking to increase their powers.

Passing the small sign that I had previously noticed, I turned to go through the threshold, looking for the entrance to the temple. As I entered the small room at the back of the store, I noticed a large number of mason jars filled with what I suspected to be various ingredients for potions and elixirs. The hundreds of strange ingredients were interesting in their own right, but this was not what I was looking for. Where was the temple? I remembered the young couple who had also asked to enter the temple ahead of me. I knew that they did not walk past me because the entrance to the back room was too small for me to miss them. Upon closer inspection, I noticed that toward the back of the store there was a door that led into a courtyard typical of those you find in the French Quarter. The courtyard's exits were locked with padlocks, so there was no way the couple could have exited without my seeing them. Just as I turned around to go back into the shop, I noticed there was a small entrance from the courtyard that led back into another part of the building—a room that was inaccessible from the voodoo shop itself. I had found the temple, and it was more than I would have ever expected.

The entrance led to a corridor that was narrow and filled with individual altars dedicated to Roman Catholic pontiffs, surrounded by bookshelves of esoteric books. These items made the narrow corridor even more restrictive. After I passed through the corridor, the room opened up, and I could finally see what was hidden inside. The room was literally full of treasure. There must have been thousands of dollars shoved in every nook and cranny of the many idols and altars that filled the room. Ones, fives, tens, twenties, fifties, and even hundred-dollar bills were cast about. Entering the room reminded me of the cartoons in which the characters find themselves among so many riches that they can do the backstroke in gold coins and precious jewels.

Voodoo Temple, Offering to St. Mary

This is just one example of a voodoo temple found in the American context that encourages the veneration of spiritual figures from multiple religious backgrounds.

In addition to currency, there were diamond rings, expensive watches, and other valuables left upon the altars. One of the most notable items in the room was a fish tank dedicated to the mermaid spirits. There was no water in this tank. Instead, it was filled with monetary gifts left as payment for spirits in an attempt to gain their favor.

MONEY FOR THE MERMAID

The gifts and offerings provided to a water spirit (mermaid) in the hope of receiving benefits from the spirit world.

As I was looking around the room, I almost failed to notice the young couple in the back corner of the temple. They were stooped down, writing their requests on a small piece of paper. I watched them as they deposited the paper into the mouth of the idol and placed a twenty-dollar bill at its feet. When they noticed me, they looked uncomfortable. They quickly walked past me as they exited the temple into the courtyard and back into the rear of the voodoo shop.

Without going into every detail about the spirits depicted upon the various altars and idols, let me say that just about every voodoo spirit I have ever heard of was represented there in the temple. The temple also included various other religious idols such as statues of the Buddha and various Hindu spirits. This temple was open to any religion; there was no competition, and all could be equally worshiped here. Moreover, they could be worshiped in any form or way the individual desired. This was a popular place, and it represented quite well the religiosity of American spirituality.

"Wow, we cannot talk about that! If we did, the worshipers who come here would fall down in fear if they knew about that. . . ."—Voodoo priestess

---

After leaving the temple, I engaged the voodoo priestess in conversation. I asked her about the significance of the temple. She answered, but due in part to her accent, her words made no sense. All that I could make out was her claim that all people are spiritual. She said, "The spirits called me and demanded that I build this temple on their behalf." She then declared, "There are many spirits in this place that the people look to for comfort and assistance." I asked her about the altars to the voodoo spirits. She responded, "Wow, we cannot talk about that! If we did, the worshipers who come here would fall down in fear if they knew about that." Somehow, this woman knew that I understood what she was really about. It was obvious that most of the visitors who find her shop have no idea of the danger that awaits them. She lures them in under the idea that all gods are the same. She teaches that all spirits can bring blessings, without explaining the truth of what is going on in her temple. While the spirituality of those who visit the temple may be generic, the spirituality of the voodoo priest is not. What appears to be a Christian symbol mixed among other religious symbols is nothing other than the same old lie of Satan, standing in for a demon as are the other idols. The prophet Isaiah warns the people of Israel about the nature of idols:

> The ironsmith takes a cutting tool and works it over the coals. He fashions it with hammers and works it with his strong arm. He becomes hungry, and his strength fails; he drinks no water and is faint. The carpenter stretches a line; he marks it out with a pencil. He shapes it with planes and marks it

with a compass. He shapes it into the figure of a man, with the beauty of a man, to dwell in a house. He cuts down cedars, or he chooses a cypress tree or an oak and lets it grow strong among the trees of the forest. He plants a cedar and the rain nourishes it. Then it becomes fuel for a man. He takes a part of it and warms himself; he kindles a fire and bakes bread. Also he makes a god and worships it; he makes it an idol and falls down before it. Half of it he burns in the fire. Over the half he eats meat; he roasts it and is satisfied. Also he warms himself and says, "Aha, I am warm, I have seen the fire!" And the rest of it he makes into a god, his idol, and falls down to it and worships it. He prays to it and says, "Deliver me, for you are my god!" (Isaiah 44:12–17)

The idols that men make are not spiritually neutral. They are items made out of wood, silver, and gold. Satan and his demons are always waiting to take advantage of man-made idols. The apostle Paul confirms this and warns of the demonic influence that they can hold:

Consider the people of Israel: are not those who eat the sacrifices participants in the altar? What do I imply then? That food offered to idols is anything, or that an idol is anything? No, I imply that what pagans sacrifice they offer to demons and not to God. I do not want you to be participants with demons. You cannot drink the cup of the Lord and the cup of demons. You cannot partake of the table of the Lord and the table of demons. (1 Corinthians 10:18–21)

Unfortunately, the world is bound to disbelieve such warnings. Scripture is no longer the norm for an American spirituality now separated from the Church. If Scripture is understood or used at all by those claiming to be spiritual but not religious, it is probably being interpreted from a purely subjective perspective. The reader determines what the text means

---

The idols that men make are not spiritually neutral.

to him and his own context rather than trusting in the way the Church has understood it for centuries. Yet, the Church was also cautioned of such a day. St. Paul warns the young Timothy:

> For the time is coming when people will not endure sound teaching, but having itching ears they will accumulate for themselves teachers to suit their own passions, and will turn away from listening to the truth and wander off into myths. (2 Timothy 4:3–4)

Paul's words are true of today's spiritual movement and stand as a warning to anyone who seeks spirituality apart from the truth of God's Holy Word.

What Do We Believe about the Dead?

In the case of spiritualism, there is usually a heavy emphasis upon communicating with the dead. That is why cemeteries hold a powerful attraction for those involved with voodoo practices. The cemeteries surrounding the French Quarter provide a clear example of the animistic practices that can be seen across America.

Cemeteries and funeral homes provide one of the clearest portals into how American spirituality views life after death. Historic St. Louis Cemetery No. 1 is one of the most popular tourist attractions in the French Quarter. The popular voodoo queen, Marie Laveau, is said to be buried there, and the cemetery is littered with offerings left to the various other voodoo personalities. Some of the items include locks of hair, pictures, charms, and even money. Sometimes people leave food offerings and candy for the spirits of the dead in an attempt to gain their favor. As strange as this may seem, these things are actually common in our society. To be sure, the practices we generally see, or even take part in, are not as blatantly occult as those found in St. Louis Cemetery No. 1. Nevertheless, similar practices are to be found right under our noses.

Scripture is no longer the norm for an American spirituality now separated from the Church.

What do most American funerals or memorials have in common with the voodoo practices found in St. Louis Cemetery No. 1? As a pastor, my responsibilities include conducting funerals. At each funeral, I stand beside the casket during the viewing and watch the people who pass by to "pay their respects" to the deceased. I listen to what they say to the dead. (Yes, people talk to the dead.) Most people simply say goodbye, but others enter into conversations that include confessing sins, asking for forgiveness, and making promises. For the most part, this is part of the grieving process and has more to do with the living than the dead. Still, sometimes there is more behind their words and actions than just grief. Rather than understanding that the soul of the dead has gone to be with the Lord, they believe that the dead are still in their midst. Some think the soul remains in the world much like a ghost; others believe the soul is still within the body. But if asked about these things, most would deny it, because they know such beliefs are contrary to the faith they profess. In truth, many people are of a divided mind. If asked, they would say they believe that the dead are with Jesus. But when observed, their actions (like placing items in the caskets with their loved ones) say something quite different.

The list of items people leave in caskets is unlimited, but they are generally personal in nature, such as pictures of the family, personal items of special importance, and sometimes even cell phones and audio players. These are things that family members provide for the comfort of the dead who will be buried. Many times, people seek to be cremated to avoid the uncomfortable thought of being buried, as if the soul remains within the body. Others think that the soul remains at the place of death. Proof of this can be found in the shrines scattered along the highways and roadways of America. Such practices are animistic in nature. They suppose that the spirits of the dead are localized but normally unseen.

Many of these people will secretly continue to speak to their dead relatives and at times even recount visits from them in the night. To be sure, this is not true of everyone who sets up shrines to the dead, but upon investigation it will be true of a great number of those who practice such venerations. While not everyone will set up roadside shrines to the dead, similar practices can be found in most cemeteries.

I must admit that I have always enjoyed walking through cemeteries. Both of my parents died in their mid-sixties, and whenever I am in the area of the cemetery in which they are buried I try to visit their graves. As I stare down at their graves, I think about the day of the resurrection and the fact that the bodies of my dear parents will someday come forth from the grave and live. Christians have always taken great care of their dead, and in doing so they confess their faith in the resurrection. We place flowers on the graves in spring, summer, and fall. And in the winter, many people place grave blankets in the snow as markers to locate the grave.

Many churches hold their Easter sunrise services in cemeteries as a reminder that just as Jesus rose from the dead, so, too, will the bodies buried in the graves that surround them. Memorial Day has also become a day when families go to cemeteries in remembrance of those who died in service to their country and other family members who have died in the past. These are good and healthy practices that should not be misunderstood.

But sometimes the focus shifts from remembrance to necromancy. Necromancy is the attempt to communicate with the dead. Such communication can take place directly or indirectly. Those who seek signs from the dead or actively seek the dead to make their presence known to them tend to fall into the trappings of spiritualism. Sometimes, the indirect forms of communications found around tombs and cemeteries are more subtle. For example, a child loved to eat candy bars, so the parents leave one next to the child's grave. When they return, they notice that the candy bar is gone, so they leave another one. Before long, they begin to do so out of devotion to the child. Maybe it is not a candy bar but money, sporting equipment, teddy bears, etc. What began as a simple act of remembrance has now become an act of veneration.

Many believe that by making gifts to the dead, the dead will in turn repay their followers with various wishes and blessings.

There is no confusion when it comes to the tombs found in St. Louis Cemetery No. 1. The tombs associated with voodoo are clearly identifiable. They are covered with gifts that include pictures, jewelry, and money inserted into the crevices of the worn tombs. On the tomb of voodoo queen Marie Laveau, I noticed a fifty-dollar bill, which had been torn in two pieces. Only half of the bill was attached to the tomb. It appeared as if the devotee had torn the bill and had left only one part of the bill to dissuade anyone from stealing the money from the tomb. These gifts are provided as payment for the requests made to the spirits at the tomb, or at times repayments for services that had been previously granted.

Tomb of Voodoo Queen Marie Laveau

This tomb is continually venerated by those who follow Marie Laveau, the high priestess of New Orleans voodoo.

The veneration of the dead is a common practice within animistic societies. In fact, many of the practices of devotion previously described mimic those of the traditional religions found in the world. One example is the tombs of Madagascar. The people of Madagascar live in extreme poverty. Their homes are normally constructed of sticks and mud. Yet, their tombs look like homes constructed to stand the test of time. Why would these people who suffer such poverty invest all of their money into their tombs when they themselves live in such meager homes? The answer is twofold. First, the people believe that they will be spending eternity in the tombs but only a short lifetime in their earthly homes. Second, the people believe that their ancestors are present in the tombs as spirits who can be contacted and encouraged to provide the living with advice, healing, and good fortune.

Animistic people do not believe in a resurrection. In fact, a resurrection of the body is not necessary for them. They instead believe that when one dies, a transition takes place. The person moves from the realm of the "living" to the realm of the "living dead." The tomb is the home that they will share with their families because it is where all of their ancestors are laid to rest. Some of the tombs have doors, windows, and courtyards.

MODERN TOMB IN NEW ORLEANS

This tomb represents some of the modern tombs found in the cemeteries surrounding the city of New Orleans.

This is a traditional tomb as found on the island of Madagascar.

The spirituality that is commonly referred to these days by those who claim to be "spiritual but not religious" is similar to that which one would find in an animistic society like Madagascar. In the next chapter, you will learn about the connection between the Western philosophy of naturalism and its connection to modern-day spiritualism.

Chapter 2 Study Questions

1. Consider the story at the beginning of the chapter about a man and his son. Did this story surprise you? Why or why not? Explain your answers.

2. What was the biblical basis for the voodoo priest's protection spell as explained in the chapter? Why is such a use of Holy Scripture inconsistent with the Christian faith?

3. The voodoo temple described in the chapter included many Christian symbols intermixed with the symbols of other religions. Why are so many people drawn to such forms of pan-spirituality?

4. Read 2 Timothy 4. How does St. Paul's warning to Timothy apply to the content of this chapter?

5. Have you ever left flowers or other items at the grave of a loved one? If so, what is the difference between the practices described in this chapter and that which you do for those who have departed?

6. What does the term *necromancy* mean? Read Leviticus 19:31; 20:6; 20:27; Deuteronomy 18:9–12; 1 John 4:1; Isaiah 8:19; 1 Timothy 4:1; and 2 Corinthians 11:14. How does God view necromancers?

People today are afraid, but this is nothing new. Humanity has always lived in fear.

CHAPTER

3

THREE COMPETING WORLDVIEWS

For the word of the cross is folly to those who are perish-
ing, but to us who are being saved it is the power of God.
(1 Corinthians 1:18)

What Is a Worldview?

What is a worldview? There are many answers to this question, but the general consensus defines a worldview as the lens by which someone organizes or structures the world. There are three popular worldviews commonly spoken of by philosophers in our time: the premodern, modern, and postmodern worldviews. But for our purposes we will focus on three different worldview categories: the animistic or spiritual worldview, the naturalistic worldview, and the biblical worldview. Before we take a closer look at American spirituality, it is necessary to understand these ways of viewing the world. Our worldview answers the basic questions of life and death. While life can be a scary endeavor, the unknown possibility of death causes many people to search for answers in dangerous places.

People today are afraid, but this is nothing new. Humanity has always lived in fear. From the Christian perspective, the perspective of this book, this fear began shortly after the creation when Adam and Eve recognized that they were naked. They had been born naked and never recognized their situation as a problem, but with the entrance of sin and death, everything changed. Sin entered the world, and with its entrance came fear. Adam and Eve were afraid just as we continue in fear. He who sins shall die (Genesis 2:17). At the heart of our common fear is death. When will we die? When will our time come? How will it come? What will happen to us when we die? What has happened to those we love? Such questions plague the unbelieving mind. Do you disagree? Maybe you do. Maybe you are one of those who rarely thinks of such things. Maybe you think science will answer the problem of death before it comes to you. Yet, even if you pretend that you are safe for the time being, crime, sickness, and the problems of this world will rip away the curtains of your false security. Death is coming. We all know it. Yet, what happens after death? Is there anything else?

At the heart of our common fear is death.

As I began writing this book, I noticed a social media post that read: "I don't subscribe to any particular religion. I'm open to the possibility of all of them. All I know is that I believe in something. What it is, I'll find out when I die." The person who wrote this post would generally be categorized as an agnostic, a person who is unsure about a belief in God or other spiritual reality. Such a person has decided to avoid the thought of death until it comes upon him. Yet, this is one of the most disturbing ways to live. The question of death remains, and fear increases as death approaches. The agnostic is prone to look for answers when faced with the problems of this life. Because such people generally avoid organized religion, they seek other "answers" as the volume of their questions increases, and they begin to tune out their disbelief. Such people could be included in those who tend to describe themselves as "spiritual but not religious." To be spiritual is to believe in something more than the "closed system of nature." Yet, by denying to be religious, such a person attempts to distance himself from any organized religious system or confession. This provides the opportunity to seek out any spiritual avenue that presents itself. While the phrase "spiritual but not religious" is common in the twenty-first century, it is not exclusive to this time period. It is actually a regressive movement that finds its roots in animism or paganism.

The Animistic or Spiritual Worldview Explained

Natural religion, otherwise known as animism, seeks to control the spiritual powers of the world for its own good. This worldview recognizes that there is a "higher power" that could be described as a god. Such a "god" is outside of the material world and has little to do with this life. Therefore, contact with this god is not a possibility. Yet, many believe there is a spiritual world that *does* interact with humanity. An animist believes that a proper management of the spirit world can bring benefits, whereas improper management can bring calamity. Not all agnostics will follow this path, but many of them do. Nevertheless, it is not just the agnostics that end up in this predicament.

Christians are now joining others who are looking for a spiritual experience or answers outside of the Christian faith. The "organized religions" these Christians are leaving are the catalysts for the change. Many in Christianity today follow an emotionally charged Christianity that seeks a more "authentic" relationship with God. The search for the authentic implies that the "organized" approach to religion is somehow less "authentic." The focus here is on the subjective—that is, the feelings and emotions that reside within oneself—rather than the objective, that which finds its source outside of the self. Traditionally, Christianity has understood humanity's connection to God in terms of God's actions toward humanity (objective), rather than humanity's actions toward God (subjective). This objective connection comes as a result of God's work of creation and His continued activity in His creation. Jesus is the ultimate end of that activity. God sent His only begotten Son to enter into creation through the incarnation.

The incarnation of Jesus eternally connected man and God together within the person of Jesus. Therefore, Christianity is understood as the action of Jesus objectively reconciling the world to God. While it carries some subjective elements such as personal faith and, at times, emotional feelings about one's faith, these subjective elements are secondary to the objective nature of the Christian faith. The defining act of God and His reconciliation of the world takes place outside of humanity in the actions of Jesus, who carried the sin of the world within His body to the cross upon which He was crucified and died and then rose from the dead on the third day. Christianity traditionally found its connection to God through outward acts or rites implemented by Jesus (i.e., preaching, the Absolution of sins, Baptism, and the Lord's Supper). These are objective Means of Grace apart from the internal subjective reception of the means. In other words, Christianity understood the work of Jesus and the benefits Christians receive to be primarily objective and only secondarily subjective. Such an understanding is dwindling these days as Christians begin looking for a more "authentic" spiritual experience. For many within the Church, the desire for something more "authentic" really means something more experiential in nature. Many would describe such an experience as a mystical or otherworldly experience.

The term *mysticism* might come to mind at this point. Mysticism has continually attempted to attach itself to the Christian experience throughout the ages. Each time its influence is felt, the Church changes its focus from the work of Jesus to individual experiences. Thus, mysticism can lead to an animistic form of Christianity that seeks to control the spiritual world in search for an authentic or emotional experience. While such activity may not always lead to animism, often those who pursue it end up on an emotional cliff.

Interaction with the spiritual world is an addictive behavior. The search for an authentic spiritual relationship is an ongoing pursuit much like that of an adrenaline junky who continues to search for greater excitement.

For many, the search begins with worship styles, then advances to ecstatic states, and ultimately leads to a desire to communicate with the spiritual realm. Many within the Western world have followed this progression. We will call this final state an animistic or spiritual worldview.

The animistic or spiritual worldview is one of the oldest of all worldviews. It can be found in ancient societies all over the world. Once again, the term *worldview* simply means the way one understands the world around him. An animistic worldview tends to accept the reality of a creator god that stands outside of his creation, a far-away god that has distanced himself from the daily workings of the world. In his stead, he has allowed for a host of lesser gods, spirits, and ancestors to rule the world. In the animistic worldview, these spiritual beings are morally neutral and, if properly satisfied, can be encouraged to use their power to advance human desires. But, if not properly managed, they can bring great calamity. Modern-day spiritualists call these spirits angel guides, elemental spirits, and deceased spirits (ghosts).

The Naturalistic Worldview

The naturalistic worldview denies any form of spiritual existence. Those who hold to a naturalistic worldview look to so-called natural causes to explain the unknown things of the world. For the naturalist, all things would require an evolutionary development. Life and death are natural events tied to a cause-and-effect relationship. For the naturalist, there is only the cosmos. Naturalism understands the cosmos to be a "closed system"—that is, a system without spiritual influences. Naturalism finds its roots in disciplines of Rationalism and the Enlightenment. Naturalism contends that the modern world is missing a functional cosmology. Therefore, it seeks to explain all spiritual phenomena in terms of a scientific model. Yet, naturalism fails to provide an adequate spirituality.[5] People recognize that something is missing, but they are unable to determine what that is.

---

5   Thomas Berry, "Classical Western Spirituality and the American Experience," *Cross Currents* (Winter 1981): 390.

[Naturalism] seeks to explain all spiritual phenomena in terms of a scientific model.

As a result of naturalism's flawed cosmology, many of those who begin with a naturalistic worldview often find their way into the philosophy of nihilism. This transition is a result of naturalism's denial of spiritual realities. If this world is all that one can expect, and death brings a cessation of life, despair is sure to follow. Nihilism is the natural result of such a deterministic philosophy. Nihilism denies the possibility of truth and ultimately finds one's own existence to be senseless. This leads many who follow nihilism into personal despair, which, left unbridled, leads to the negation of personal morals and in many instances to suicide. This is the problem of over-humanization; it expresses an "ultimate confidence in humanity."[6] Such a view of humanity has constantly failed to provide a successful answer to the problems of the world. From a biblical perspective, the doctrine of original sin enlightens us to the problem. Sin has corrupted all that God has created. St. Paul reminds us:

> For we know that the whole creation has been groaning together in the pains of childbirth until now. And not only the creation, but we ourselves, who have the firstfruits of the Spirit, groan inwardly as we wait eagerly for adoption as sons, the redemption of our bodies. For in this hope we were saved. Now hope that is seen is not hope. For who hopes for what he sees? But if we hope for what we do not see, we wait for it with patience. (Romans 8:22–25)

When one lacks an understanding of original sin and seeks after utopia on earth, the problems of such a worldview will not be far behind. People will begin to ask themselves the question, "Is this all there is?" Humans cannot live without a sense of personal worth. Naturalism does not provide any worth to the individual. In the end, naturalists will either be faced

---

6   Jeff B. Pool, "Toward Spirituality of Post-Christian Disciples of Jesus," *Communio Viatorum* 53, no. 1 (2011): 12.

with the hopelessness of nihilism, or they will eventually find their way back into an animistic or spiritual worldview. American culture is beginning to come full circle from naturalism/modernism to postmodernism, which leads to an openness to almost any possibility, with the exception of the biblical worldview.

The Biblical Worldview

In the biblical worldview, the true God is not a far-away or unattached creator. He is the One who holds all things together in Christ Jesus (Colossians 1:17). God the Father seeks worshipers from His creation (John 4:23–24). God remains connected to His creation in a special way. He becomes man and dwells with His creation in the person of Jesus the Christ. Jesus is true God, and as a result of the incarnation, He is at the same time true man. God is so connected to His creation that He took the sin of all creation into His sinless body and died for the sin of the world. After three days of being entombed, He took up His life and rose from the dead. The ultimate end of those who die is presented in the reality of the resurrection. All will bodily rise on the Last Day, the evil and the good (Acts 24:15). What about the intermediary state between death and the resurrection? The Bible acknowledges an intermediary state of consciousness but tells us very little of what that state will be like with the exception that it will be better for the Christian than the current life that is attached to sin and death (see Philippians 1:23). Instead of focusing on the intermediate state between death and the resurrection, the Bible's focus is always upon the resurrection.

> Nihilism denies the possibility of truth and ultimately finds one's own existence to be senseless.

A belief in the spirits of the dead or ghosts is not within a biblical worldview. The scriptural evidence is clear: "It is appointed for man to die once, and after that comes judgment" (Hebrews 9:27). Likewise, Philippians 1:23 is clear that when Christians die, they go to be with Jesus, which we are told "is far better" than living in the fallen world. Therefore, the suggestion that there is a realm of the spirits in which they remain active in the world after death is excluded. In other words, there are no ghosts. It is true that on a few occasions the spirits of the departed have shown themselves. One of the most cited examples by spiritualists is the appearance of Moses and Elijah with Jesus on the Mount of Transfiguration (Matthew 17:1–13; Mark 9:2–8; Luke 9:28–36; 2 Peter 1:16–18). Nevertheless, this example has nothing to do with ghosts; instead, it refers to the intermediary state between death and the resurrection. This is not too unlike that which St. Paul referred to in Philippians 1:23. Both of the great prophets of the Old Testament who appear alongside Jesus at the Mount of Transfiguration are awaiting the resurrection. The transfiguration should not be seen as a proof text for ghosts but as a picture of heaven breaking through and touching the earth. Wherever Jesus is, so, too, is the whole company of heaven. The great prophets at Jesus' side are not wandering spirits walking the earth but representatives of the souls of all those who, while currently residing in heaven, are awaiting the day of their resurrection.

The other example referred to by spiritualists is the spirit of Samuel in the Old Testament (1 Samuel 28:7–19). Biblical scholars continue to argue over the significance of this text. They struggle with the identity and nature of the spirit of Samuel depicted in the text. Is the spirit truly Samuel, or is it a demonic deception? If it is Samuel, does such a text imply the existence of ghosts? If 1 Samuel 28 is taken at face value, then it was truly the spirit of the prophet that appeared to condemn King Saul. But the text also makes it clear that the spirit speaks on behalf of God, and the spirit is sent for that specific purpose. It is my contention that this story in no way implies a wandering, disembodied spirit but a special situation much like that which was seen in the transfiguration event.

The Bible teaches us that in the spiritual realm there are only two categories of spirits: holy angels and the fallen angels—otherwise known as demons. Holy Scripture has numerous examples of how the holy angels are used by God in His creation. These angels never work at the command of humanity but only on behalf of God as both His messengers and His warriors. On the other hand, the fallen angels constantly seek to lead humanity away from God and destroy His creation. The leader of these fallen angels is named Satan, otherwise known as the devil. He is called the father of lies (John 8:44) and through his deceptions humanity is continually led astray.

The Bible warns us not to attempt to contact the dead nor engage in communications with spiritual beings. Those who break this command are referred to as necromancers. The biblical worldview denies the animistic or spiritual worldview commonly found in our time, while at the same time, it is accepting of the existence of God, angels, and demons.

Postmodernism: Spiritual but Not Religious

Postmodernism is a philosophy that makes an outward denial of objective truth, including the truth of naturalism, Christianity, or any other system that would claim it possesses ultimate truth. Nevertheless, most people recognize that there is something more than the physical world. Because of their lack of trust in organizations and institutions, postmodernists have disconnected their spirituality from religion in the formal sense. The spiritualist finds his ultimate meaning in his own experiences apart from the experiences of anyone else.[7] Such an individualistic spirituality claims to provide for a personal relationship with the divine. Moreover, such a self-centered theology allows for the divine to be whatever or whomever the individual chooses to attach his allegiance to.[8] With secularization's dismissal of institutional religious affiliation and its acceptance of the various religious traditions, American spirituality provides an open invitation to experience whatever spirituality the individual can recognize within the world or the self.[9] "Spiritual people" have no need to acknowledge a source of ultimate knowledge or truth—they find the truth within themselves. With such a worldview, any philosophy can be merged together with any other philosophy or religion as long as the person finds

---

7   Adam McClendon, "Defining the Role of the Bible in Spirituality: 'Three Degrees of Spirituality' in American Culture," *Journal of Spiritual Formation and Soul Care* 5, no. 2 (September 2012): 208.

8   Adam McClendon, "Defining the Role of the Bible in Spirituality: 'Three Degrees of Spirituality' in American Culture," 211.

9   Eric Michael Mazur and Kate McCarthy, "Part 3: Popular Spirituality and Morality," in *God in the Details: American Religion in Popular Culture* (New York: Routledge, 2001), 177.

self-fulfillment in that particular worldview. While such a worldview appears to demonstrate a form of chronic individualism, these so-called "personal experiences" eventually become a shared dogma of syncretic faiths.[10] As it turns out, personal experience is not really all that personal. As the so-called "spiritual but not religious" groups interact, they begin to recognize their shared experiences.

The transformation from naturalism to spiritualism is most clearly demonstrated in today's paranormal subculture. I first recognized this when I had the opportunity to be a guest on a number of prominent paranormal radio programs after writing my first book, *I Am Not Afraid: Demon Possession and Spiritual Warfare*.[11] What I found amazing about these programs was the desire of their audiences to accept almost any possibility regarding spiritual things. However, when confronted with answers from the perspective of a biblical worldview that accepts the Scriptures as the true Word of God, their spiritual openness disappeared, and they became antagonist and closed-minded. This is especially true of those who are involved in paranormal investigation.

A paranormal investigator is someone who believes in numerous spiritual realities and seeks to prove their existence through scientific means. If you are not aware of these groups, you have not been paying attention to the American spiritual climate. The paranormal has taken over cable television's documentary channels. Such television stations feature stories of so-called true haunting, paranormal activity, ghost encounters, mediums, and a host of other shows that fall into similar categories. Before becoming mainstream, this type of show had maintained a prominent position on late-night radio. Today, one of the most common places that the paranormal subculture can be found is on social media, especially on Facebook and Twitter.

---

10 Peter Versteeg and Johan Roeland, "Contemporary Spirituality and the Making of Religious Experience: Studying the Social in an Individualized Religiosity," *Fieldwork in Religion* 6, no. 2 (2012): 124.

11 Robert H. Bennett, *I Am Not Afraid: Demon Possession and Spiritual Warfare: True Accounts from the Lutheran Church of Madagascar* (St. Louis: Concordia, 2013).

People today are afraid, but this is nothing new. Humanity has always lived in fear.

Is American spirituality afraid? Simply watch one of these programs, and the answer will become clear. Modern-day society lives in fear. With the decline in modernity and the rise of postmodernism, people are required to form new ways of understanding their world. They are reverting to a form of religious paganism that is the basis of all tribal and animistic worldviews. As a result of this transformation of Western culture, people are making a mass exodus from the pews of traditional churches.

Why are these people leaving their churches? Many people have attempted to answer this question, but I find the answers of Jeff Pool helpful. Pool is the Eli Lilly Chair of Religion and Culture and Professor of Religion at Berea College in Berea, Kentucky. He finds four primary reasons why people leave structured religious institutions and seek personal religiosity. (1) Religion has lost itself. (2) People seek to lose themselves from what they believe to be an oppressive, distorted, immoral, and destructive faith. (3) To lose "religion" provides one the opportunity to liberate oneself from one's "self-imposed oppression." (4) People want to lose "religion" because of its ignorance.[12]

Many churches have accepted a theological pluralism (an acceptance of diverse theological belief) that can also be described as spiritualism. But the spiritualist worldview that has become prominent in today's churches is nothing new to Christianity. The Christian Church has existed in the midst of pluralistic religious environments since its establishment by Jesus and the sending out of His disciples. All of the creeds and confessions of historic Christianity are in response to the heresies of history. The difference between the churches of the past and the churches of today lies in their response to attacks, which are increasing with ever-growing

---

12 Jeff B. Pool, "Toward Spirituality of Post-Christian Disciples of Jesus," *Communio Viatorum* 53, no. 1 (2001): 14.

frequency. Rather than continuing to provide a place of sanctuary from the lies of Satan, his demons, and the world, many churches have embraced a concept of personal experience that overshadows divine revelation. In a sense, churches have let the demonic genie out of the bottle and welcomed him into the church. This became evident in the church-growth movement, which sought to make worship "more relevant" so as to bring more people into the church. As a result of focusing on personal comfort and experience, the church-growth movement replaced (or at least added to) the truths of Scripture with modern marketing techniques connected to the social sciences. Other churches have chosen a different path, a path void of creeds and doctrines.

One of the most anticreedal church bodies within the American context is the Southern Baptist Church. At the heart of the Southern Baptist ethos is the doctrine of "soul competency." The doctrine of soul competency requires that individualistic precedence is placed over creedal acceptance. Individualistic precedence finds truth in the heart of the individual through the action of the Holy Spirit. Such Spirit knowledge is believed to be God-given and thus something that can exist without a prescribed dogma (teaching) or confession. Soul competency is "the God-given freedom and ability of persons to know and respond to God's will."[13] Basically, the thought follows the argument that the Holy Spirit can reveal various truths to various people. Therefore, no single creedal statement can be trusted to fit every experience. When taken to its logical conclusions, this doctrine destroys the possibility of confessional subscription and allows for various interpretations to exist side by side within the Church. The problems such an inconsistent theology can bring to those within the Church who have minimal biblical knowledge should be evident: inconsistency leads to anxiety during times of personal struggles, and anxiety leads to fear. The Christian faith is not one of fear nor is it an inconsistent faith. God has spoken to us by His prophets, and now in these last days He speaks to us through His Son (Hebrews 1:1–2).

---

13 Baptist Distinctives, "Is Soul Competency *The* Baptist Distinctive?," baptistdistinctives.org/articles/is-soul-competency-the-baptist-distinctive/ (accessed May 19, 2014).

Pool's second point speaks to the problem of dogma without grace. He finds that people seek to free themselves from what they perceive as an oppressive religion. Such a statement can be interpreted many ways, but I think it best refers to a Christianity that has lost the Gospel. The Lutheran Church confesses a theology of presence. We trust that where the Word of God is proclaimed and the Sacraments are administered according to Jesus' institution, Jesus promises to be present with His people as One who provides forgiveness and life to the sinner. When the presence of Jesus within the rites of the Church are not understood or are rejected, Christianity becomes an institution focused on moralism and self-help strategies rather than a place of release and forgiveness. Moralism is the belief that one can gain access to God through personal effort. Churches that hold to heavy forms of moralism cause their members to search for freedom. Such a search that is disconnected from Jesus leads many to seek out the spiritual movement that is now prevalent in our society. Spiritualism promises complete and personal freedom from religious institutions, but it leads only to greater oppression.

The search for personal freedom also leads to Pool's next point: many people leave religion because they want to free themselves from themselves. As I was writing this book, I noticed that a number of news programs were covering a story about a woman who had decided to upload a video to YouTube documenting her abortion. She stated that her intention was to remove the shame that many women experience as a result of making the decision to abort their children. On the video, she discusses the shame that she said she once had concerning abortion. She presents her abortion as a beautiful work of art rather than the horrific dismembering of an innocent life. She chose this opportunity to liberate herself from her own "self-imposed oppression." She embraced what she knew to be a sin so

---

Where the Word of God is proclaimed and the Sacraments are administered according to Jesus' institution, Jesus promises to be present with His people.

---

that it would no longer feel like a sin. Our sinful nature continually seeks to justify itself even if this self-justification requires one to turn his back on the truth and fall prey to a lie.

The final reason Pool suggests people are leaving the institutional church is what he calls an attempt to lose its ignorance. I take this to mean the ridiculousness of what goes on in today's megachurches. At the time of this writing, Lakewood Church, led by Joel and Victoria Osteen in Houston, Texas, is the largest church in America. The message presented by the Osteens is not unique; it is spoken in similar ways by many American Evangelical leaders and churches. The Osteens' message is more about the people they are preaching to than it is about Jesus or His promises. To be blunt, this is a church that is unrecognizable to the churches of the New Testament period. It is the "church of me" rather than the Church of Jesus. Such a church provides a logical journey from an orthodox, confessional, theological Christianity into the pool of American spirituality.

American Spirituality: A Lost Worldview

If you have found this chapter to be confusing, then you're beginning to understand the mess of American spirituality. When God and His means of providing grace are removed from the focus of one's heart, what follows will eventually lead back to the father of lies. While such a statement may seem overly simplistic for some, it does have a biblical basis. In 1 Corinthians, Paul writes:

> Let no one deceive himself. If anyone among you thinks that he is wise in this age, let him become a fool that he may become wise. For the wisdom of this world is folly with God. For it is written, "He catches the wise in their craftiness," and again, "The Lord knows the thoughts of the wise, that they are futile." (3:18–20)

Paul is not promoting anti-intellectualism. Actually, for him, wisdom is something to aspire to. However, wisdom apart from the revealed Word of God is not wisdom but a lie. Such a false wisdom is due to spiritual darkness. It is demonically imposed upon fallen humanity by the evil spiritual forces and the devil. Such is Paul's point in the Epistle to the Colossians, where he writes, "See to it that no one takes you captive by philosophy and empty deceit, according to human tradition, according to the elemental spirits of the world, and not according to Christ" (2:8).

The elemental spirits to which Paul refers are demons that seek to turn God's created children into false worship through means of philosophy. In the context of Colossians, the Greek word *philosophia*, or philosophy, literally means "a love for wisdom." Wisdom is a desirable trait, but false wisdom is not from God, and anything not from God is a lie.

Satan, sin, and death reside at the heart of a fallen worldview. Once again, St. Paul is clear on this point. In Ephesians 2, he describes the problem of a fallen humanity and ultimate allegiance of those who are in the darkness of disbelief:

> And you were dead in the trespasses and sins in which you once walked, following the course of this world, following the prince of the power of the air, the spirit that is now at work in the sons of disobedience—among whom we all once lived in the passions of our flesh, carrying out the desires of the body and the mind, and were by nature children of wrath, like the rest of mankind. But God, being rich in mercy, because of the great love with which He loved us, even when we were dead in our trespasses, made us alive together with Christ—by grace you have been saved—and raised us up with Him and seated us with Him in the heavenly places in Christ Jesus, so that in the coming ages He might show the immeasurable riches of His grace in kindness toward us in Christ Jesus. For by grace you have been saved through faith. And this is not your own doing; it is the gift of God, not a result of works, so that no one may boast. For we are His workmanship, created in Christ Jesus for good works, which God prepared beforehand, that we should walk in them. (vv. 1–10)

At the center of the naturalistic or spiritual worldview lays sin and death. What appears to be wisdom is a facade. St. Paul's explanation for a supposed wisdom apart from the revealed truth of God is spiritual death. Dead things have no ability to act. Likewise, the spiritually dead cannot understand the things of God. Those who remain doubtful of how Scripture views the wisdom of fallen humanity simply need to continue reading the numerous scriptural verses that make this point clear. One of the more helpful verses for understanding this concept comes from 1 Corinthians:

> The natural person does not accept the things of the Spirit of God, for they are folly to him, and he is not able to understand them because they are spiritually discerned. The spiritual person judges all things, but is himself to be judged by no one. "For who has understood the mind of the Lord so as to instruct him?" But we have the mind of Christ. (2:14–16)

The natural person to whom St. Paul refers in his epistle is one who views the world apart from faith in Christ Jesus. Paul's theology is consistent. A worldview that lacks the spiritual eyes of faith will always be self-serving and at its heart follow a demonically imposed will. What will such a world look like? The answer to this question will vary depending upon one's worldview. In an animistic worldview, spirit worship and necromancy will be the norm. In areas with a Rationalistic worldview, like in the Western world, including the United States of America, science will be the norm. It is the contention of this book that in the end, both worldviews share the same lie and end up in the same place apart from the wisdom of God.

Earlier in this book, the point was made that there are only two religions. The first is false religion based on human works and satanic-induced ignorance. The second is the only true religion, which is based only on the ministry, death, and resurrection of Jesus. One of the benefits of this book is that it analyzes the effects of both religions by telling the stories of real people who have been rescued from the darkness and death of the first religion and brought to the peaceful life of forgiveness and eternity promised by Jesus Christ.

Chapter 3 Study Questions

1. Describe the three most popular worldviews found within American society.

2. What do you think is at the heart of the fears most people face?

3. In your own words, how would you describe animism? What aspects of animism have you noticed around you this week?

4. Describe objective justification. How does the doctrine of objective justification differ from subjective justification?

5. In view of what you have read in this chapter, how do you view the topic of ghosts? Has this chapter changed your mind? Why or why not?

6. Does 1 Samuel 28:7–19 prove the existence of ghosts?

7. Why would a naturalist deny the possibility of miracles?

8. What does it mean to describe one's faith as "spiritual but not religious"? Is such a view of faith compatible with the Christian faith demonstrated in the pages of Holy Scripture? Explain your answer.

9. What is the doctrine of soul competency? What difficulties does this chapter find with such a doctrine?

10. One of the reasons people give for leaving the Church is the oppressive nature they find in the dogmas of the Church. Do you agree or disagree with their concerns? Explain your answer.

American Indian
cultural expression
focuses on interact-
ing with the dead.

CHAPTER

4

American Indian Religions

You cannot drink the cup of the Lord and the cup of demons.
(1 Corinthians 10:21)

During my time as a pastor in northern Michigan, I served in an area that was heavily influenced by American Indian culture. The American Indian casino was one of the largest employers in the area. Because of both the economy and the culture, many of the members of a local church were influenced by the American Indian community in one way or another. Multicultural situations like this always influence churches. Yet while many people today encourage multiculturalism, it often brings into the Christian Church teachings that are at odds with

Christian doctrine and truth. In this particular community, this multicultural influence had penetrated the church's parochial school.

The Christian school, like many Christian schools, had a yearly talent show for the community. Like many talent shows, singing, dancing, and various other activities were included. But because of the local culture, some of the students performed American Indian rituals as part of the show. You may be thinking, "So what's the problem?" If you come from a naturalist worldview, you would probably not see a problem. If you come from a Christian worldview, you will recognize what this means.

Is It Only a Question of Culture?

The following story relates a situation that occurs daily in a beautiful resort in the mountains surrounding Tucson, Arizona. This particular resort, like many in the western parts of the United States, has an American Indian theme. In keeping with the theme, the decorations include various murals made of feathers. In the center of the courtyard, benches surround a fire pit. And each morning, the guests are encouraged to gather there to begin their day with an American Indian spiritual healing ceremony.

American Indian Healing Ceremony

American tourists gather around an American Indian shaman as he leads them through a ritual of blessing and communion with the cult of the ancestors.

AFRAID

The ceremony begins as the sun rises in the east. The American Indian shaman is dressed in his traditional garb as he welcomes his new followers. The participants all gather in the darkness around the fire, encircling the flames. The shaman begins with these words, "All people and animals and plants are of the same family, and we must respect them. This includes the ground water and Mother Earth—all are sacred." He then begins to play the flute. He explains to his followers that the flute is the traditional instrument used to call the attention of the spiritual ancestors from the world of the dead. Surrounding the Indian medicine man are pictures of his dead ancestors. As he continues to play his flute, he calls upon his ancestors. He burns incense around the fire thereby providing a pleasant smell that adds to the spiritual experience for those in attendance. Following the lengthy melodic and trance-inducing music, the shaman tells his followers about what he calls "the continuation of life."

For the American Indian shaman, life is about spirit. There is spirit in all things; therefore, all things have life within them. He goes on to claim that death is just a transformation into the spirit world. The spirit world he speaks of has no place for heaven or hell but is a continuation of life in a new spiritual plane of existence. His understanding of this spiritual existence is similar to what one might find in most spiritualistic philosophies. The dead are still in the midst of the living. They can provide assistance to their living ancestors or bring harm upon them. One way to insure their assistance is to recognize their presence and establish contact with them. The ritual of playing the flute and burning the sage, which the shaman had demonstrated previously, was not intended to simply call his own ancestors but also to demonstrate to his new initiates how they could interact with their own ancestors.

Once the shaman has explained the process of calling one's ancestors, he encourages his guests to follow him in calling their ancestors to gather

---

The spirit world he speaks of has no place for heaven or hell but is a continuation of life in a new spiritual plane of existence.

---

with them around the fire. Without exception, the tourists follow his advice and begin to participate in the service. They receive sage from the shaman and light it from the flames of the communal fire. Each of the participants are encouraged to form a prayer circle as they burn the sage and bring their individual ancestors in the presence of the gathering.

The shaman is not only concerned with calling the ancestors. He also wishes to invoke the presence of what he calls the creator. He tells those gathered around the fire that the creator of all things and the ancestors are in communion with each other. Therefore, the ancestors can bring any requests one has directly to the creator, whom the shaman calls Mother Earth. The shaman returns to his flute as the people join in silence with the burning sage in their hands. They have closed their eyes now. Each of them listens to the flute and breathes in the smell of the sage that fills their nostrils. As the new followers pray, a group of wild pigs come down to lap up the water that has condensed on the pavement. The shaman sees the pigs and explains that it is a sign from the ancestors that they have heard the prayers of the worshipers. Now that the shaman is assured that the ancestors are present, he has each of the tourists mentally cast their desires to something that appears to resemble a stringlike material. As the material burns, the shaman explains to the people that the ancestors are now carrying their prayer requests to Mother Earth. Taking a feather out of his sack, the shaman lights it from the fire. He passes the burning feather over each of their heads as if to anoint them with its power. He explains that through this ritual the evil spirits that have been lurking around them will be cast away, and they will be free from the bondage of darkness.

Following the ritual, the shaman takes the time to have a debriefing session with those who have just undergone what is in reality an exorcism. The shaman teaches the guests that his spirituality is the same as all spirituality no matter what the culture and that all people worship the same god in different ways. He encourages the tourists to be more open to the spirituality that surrounds them and the various spirits that serve as guardians over the regions of the earth.

The makeshift followers who have just been catechized by the American Indian shaman are mostly Anglo Christians. They do not share an American Indian ancestry. They are not acting out their cultural heritage. They are basically no different from most of your neighbors. Moreover, those who have just participated in calling upon their dead ancestors for blessings and who have received the shaman's exorcism consider themselves to be Christians. This is what American spirituality looks like in the twenty-first century. It still reports itself to be "Christian," but at the same time it is open to a pan-spirituality. In previous centuries, this type of spirituality would have been recognized as paganism or heresy. In our day, such a syncretistic or mixed spirituality has become common within the Christian community.

When Christians allow for this type of mixed spirituality, the Gospel becomes obscured. If blessings can be obtained through the spiritual world, apart from the love of Jesus and His sacrificial death and glorious resurrection, the need for Jesus becomes marginalized. Spiritualism and the Gospel cannot exist side by side. One of the main points of spiritualism, whether it is found in American culture, traditional animistic cultures, or American Indian cultural expression, focuses on interacting with the dead or other spiritual forces. The Bible condemns such activity as necromancy (Deuteronomy 18:10–12).

While many who practice American Indian spirituality do so for cultural reasons, Christians must recognize the danger such activity can cause. Due to our fallen nature, we are easily mislead by the world, our flesh, and the devil. Although the unbelieving world accepts American Indian spirituality and actions as cultural, Christian culture must be formed by the Holy Scriptures. The promise of the resurrection is a promise of eternal life in a re-created world that is no longer affected by sin. In contrast, the spirit world associated with American Indian religion has no place for heaven or hell but is a continuation of life in a new spiritual plane of existence. While St. Paul's warning to the Corinthians seems stern and even unloving to those who practice spiritualism, it remains an essential scriptural warning to Christians throughout time. Any worship that is disconnected from the Word of God is disconnected from Jesus and is therefore pagan. To such pagans, Paul wrote: "I imply that what pagans sacrifice they offer to demons and not to God. I do not want you to be participants with demons. You cannot drink the cup of the Lord and the cup of demons" (1 Corinthians 10:20–21).

Chapter 4 Study Questions

1. What is your view of American Indian culture? Is it compatible with Christianity? Explain your answer.

2. Have you ever participated in an American Indian ceremony like the one described in this chapter? If so, how did your experience compare to the story in this chapter?

3. The story the Indian shaman taught his hearers claimed that all religions are connected to the same God. Is such a statement true? Explain your answer.

4. Now that you have read this chapter, what thoughts do you have about including various aspects of American Indian religious practices in the worship of the Church?

At the beating heart of our sinful condition is the desire to be gods . . . we have fallen prey to the prince of this world.

CHAPTER

5

The Problems of Video Gaming and the Internet

You shall have no other gods before Me. (Exodus 20:3)

The Games We Play or the Games That Play Us?

I used to enjoy playing the video game *Age of Empires*. At the beginning of the game, civilization consists of one or two people. As you build resources, you also increase your ability to propagate the civilization. Before long, you are adding various workers, military units, and civil and religious institutions. You become godlike as you direct the will of your people in any direction of your choosing. Do you want an unarmed civilian to attack the armed forces of another society? Just send the poor shepherd out to his death, and he will follow. You are not the only god-like being; you will also be playing against the computer program, or if you choose the online version, other people will join you. Before long, you and the other territorial deities are fighting a spiritual battle through the cyber-subjects you direct. The easiest way to win the game is to create temples and then add priests, who then become your servants. Once you have enough priests to help propagate your new religion, you can direct them to convert the other societies. Your priests also have the ability to heal and even kill upon your command. As you advance, you learn key phrases by which you can miraculously speak resources into existence or destroy the other civilization with a mere word.

Okay, this is a fantasy game, so what's the problem? Nothing, and yet everything. These games develop critical-thinking skills that are helpful for modern life. But they can also become alternate realities for the person playing the game. I remember playing the game for hours that seemed to pass by like seconds. Before long, half the day, and then the entire day, would pass me by. The game was fun. At some point, I recognized that when I was playing the game I checked out from the world around me. I ignored my wife, family, and my other responsibilities as father, husband, and, yes, even pastor. If I only played the game on rare occasions, everything would be fine, but the game would always draw me in. It became an alternative reality, or as the mental health establishment would call it, a dissociative event.

Our society loves to dissociate itself from everyday life filled with the problems of the day. Some do this through mind-altering drugs and alcohol, others seek dissociation through meditation and trance. The possibilities are almost endless. People seek to find ways to escape this life because they are afraid. They are afraid of what might happen to themselves or to someone they love. They are afraid of success, and they fear failure. They are afraid of the physical and spiritual realities of life.

Gaming Spiritually

"Watch out for those games and the Internet." You hear these kinds of things all the time. Christians become concerned about many aspects of life; video gaming and Internet addictions are just two more worries that have been added to the Christian's watch list. Many times when we hear these things, we roll our eyes and maybe even think to ourselves, "There goes those overbearing Pietists again." While this may often be the case, we would be misguided if we failed to recognize the problems both video games and Internet addictions have brought upon many Christians, especially children.

I recently spoke with a mother who believed that her son had become demon possessed through video gaming. This was a wonderful Christian family who struggled with the addiction of their adult child, a brilliant student who received a full scholarship to attend a Christian institution. The student went off to school like many other children every year, ready to begin studies and prepare for a future career. He moved into the dorm room (in this case, a private room) with all of his belongings, including a computer, large screen monitor, and gaming gadgets. All of these, if used properly, can assist a student in research, entertainment, and provide a release for the homesickness that comes in the late hours of the night. Yet, just as everything in God's creation can be understood to be a gracious gift of the Creator, so, too, can everything in creation be turned into a mechanism for sin and death.

Although playing video games does not bring about imminent physical death, it can, like anything else in this world, be used as a tool of evil. The young man became addicted to playing a particular video game and became well known within the video gaming subculture. Over time, his addiction became so strong that he no longer left his room. His mother described him as having a strange look in his eyes and seemingly possessed. He quit going to class and rarely left his gaming chair. Eventually, he required treatment. (Yes, there is a treatment program for those addicted to video games. It is a residential program that is becoming more common than most people realize.)

Was this man possessed? Most of the time, there is no way of knowing the answer to such questions. Yet, following his treatment, it was not long before he returned to church. There was no formal exorcism performed upon him. There are no sensational Hollywood stories to tell. No movie deals are waiting to be signed. No, this man's healing came by means of the Word of Jesus and the power of doctors, nurses, and other people living out their vocations.

Most of the time, spiritual healing takes place in ways the world finds to be unimpressive. Our God uses the things of His creation as His means to bring about spiritual changes. In Genesis, God declared all things to be good. The cosmos, and all that it contained, was perfect. There was no evil but only good—that is, until sin entered into creation through the pride of a creature. This creature was one of the most beautiful of all angels, and his name was Lucifer. This splendid, holy angel of God's creation chose to inject his own sin of pride into the prideless creation of God. He became Satan, the father of lies. Cast out of heaven, Satan took one-third of the angels with him and became the leader of those fallen angels, all of which now carry the title of demons. But Satan and his demons are only creatures. They do not have the powers of the Creator. They cannot speak matter into existence. They have absolutely no creative power at all. Therefore, the best they can muster is to corrupt that which God created to be good.

As a result of sin, everything in the cosmos changed. St. Paul reminds us that the creation is lost in bondage and decay (Romans 8:19–23). As a result of sin, everything that has been created now bares the marks of sin. Think about this for a moment. What sin can you think of that does not involve the use of something that God created to be good? God created everything to be good so that through its use it would show His glory. So how do these good things become evil? St. Paul answers this question in Romans 1 when he describes how God turns His sinful creation over to the depravity of their own minds to do things that should not be done. A fallen society begins to worship the creation rather than the Creator (Romans 1:18–29).

The sinful acts of all creation are connected to the work of the devil. Because of sin, all people throughout history have participated in the fall through their desire to live apart from God's will. Surely, not everyone desires to turn their back on God, and not everyone has a depraved mind, do they? Scripture is clear that we are all born dead to God and to His good desires (Ephesians 2:1–3). Therefore, by nature (that is, our sinful nature), we constantly find ourselves at odds with God's will. Moreover, we are easy targets for the devil and his demons, especially when we fail to recognize our own sin and the devil's desire to destroy us (1 Peter 5:8). When at war, a good general will always expect an attack. If his foe is crafty, the general expects that he will look for a time of weakness and lack of readiness so as to inflict the greatest casualties and maybe even gain the victory.

Gaming and Internet addictions stem from the desire to turn away from God and create lesser gods to serve the individual. These desires can prevent us from properly serving our neighbors. Apart from popular belief, no one has been placed on this earth simply to search out self-fulfillment. Indeed, the search for self-fulfillment leads to sin and death in the end. The purpose of each individual's life is just the opposite. God has created us to serve, not to be served.

Our service is carried out in what is called vocation. Each of us has a vocation. Vocations include the jobs we hold as a result of our employment. Vocations include our roles as father, mother, child, spouse, and every worldly estate that has been created by God. As we serve our neighbor, we indirectly serve our Lord God, whom we find in the face of our neighbor. Likewise, through the vocation of our neighbor—through their service to us—God provides for our needs. This was the case with the young man. God released him from the hands of the evil one by serving him through the workers at the residential treatment center he attended. While such a service does not appear to be worthy of most people's notice, it is nevertheless God's activity in the world. Wherever God is acting, His activities should not be overlooked.

There was more to this man's healing than just the residential program he attended. He was also served through the vocations of his parents and his pastor. But God serves His creation through other means as well. He serves us through gifts to which He has attached Himself with His promise. The young man received these gifts in his church. As a result of the treatment he received through the vocation of the therapists, he remembered the promises that he had forgotten. These were the promises that Jesus had made to him when he was baptized, the promise that Jesus would never leave him nor forsake him (Matthew 28:20), the promise of life and salvation. The means by which God had promised to serve him were His Word and His Sacraments, the very marks of the Church by which all mankind is saved.

The vocation that God uses in the Church to administer His gifts is found in the Office of the Holy Ministry. The pastor serves God's people as the one whom God has appointed to deliver and administer the holy things of God to His holy people. To be sure, these people are sinners, but they are at the same time declared to be holy by God because of the crucifixion and resurrection of Jesus. They are holy because they carry the promise of God in the name they have received in their Baptism. The pastor serves a different vocation than that of counselors and therapists. The pastor's vocation is one of delivering the Word and the Sacraments. While pastors may have some of the abilities found in vocations like the mental health field, the focus of the Holy Ministry is upon Jesus and His service to the Church. The power of the pastor does not reside in his ability, charisma, or even academic abilities, although these are often useful gifts. No, the power of the pastor resides in the words he speaks. When a pastor is serving a church through faithful proclamation of Jesus' Word, there is Jesus in the midst of the congregation. When Absolution is proclaimed, Jesus is there forgiving sins. When Baptisms are performed, Jesus is there through the work of the Holy Spirit connecting people to His cross and resurrection. When the pastor preaches, Jesus speaks. When the pastor presides over the Lord's Supper, Jesus is there in and under the bread and wine.

The power is not found in the pastor but in the powerful presence of Jesus, who has promised to connect Himself to these simple means. While churchly things appear to be plain and almost too simple, the Church is the place where Jesus has promised to be present among His people. While it was through the mental health services that the young man came face-to-face with the addictive nature of his sin, it was only by reconnecting with the Church that he found the only relevant answer to his problem. The answer is Jesus and His promise of forgiveness and life. Where Jesus is, Satan and his demons must flee. Exorcism goes on around us all the time, too often without us ever knowing it. Exorcism and spiritual warfare are present wherever Jesus resides. This will become clearer as you continue to read this book.

Although this section of the book began with a story of a young man addicted to playing a video game, the circumstances of this chapter could have focused on almost any addiction. Addiction is a result of our sinful condition. Satan and his demons are masterful at attacking humanity in its weakness. The young man in our story was attacked through video gaming. Others may play video games repetitively with no harm. Some may be prescribed pain medicines for medical conditions and walk away with the benefits of such a treatment, but others receiving the same treatment might become addicted. Some might drink small amounts of alcoholic beverages daily with no effects, while others might become quickly addicted. Such a list could go on to describe every action in God's creation. Each individual suffers with his or her own particular propensity for sin. Yet, in each case the answer remains the same. It is an answer contrary to what we want it to be.

At the beating heart of our sinful condition is the desire to be gods and to find the answer in ourselves. But in our desire to be gods, we have fallen prey to the prince of this world—namely, Satan. The answer for a lost world is never found within oneself. The occult, mysticism, divination, or magical arts all have us looking in the wrong place for the answers. The

---

. . .the power of the pastor resides in the words he speaks. When a pastor is serving the church through faithful proclamation of Jesus' Word, there is Jesus in the midst of the congregation.

---

answer for our sin is found only in Jesus, who is serving His world through the gifts of godly vocations, both outside and inside the Church. Each of these vocations brings different gifts and promises. Our God is a God of means. The problem we face in our American spiritual climate is that we have forgotten these means and have gone looking for answers in the creation rather than the Creator. May the Lord bring us out of the spiritual darkness and into the light of His presence.

Chapter 5 Study Questions

1. How do some video games appeal to our common sinful condition?

2. Is it acceptable for a Christian to play video games like the one described in the story? Explain your answer.

3. What are your thoughts about the man described in the story? Was he facing a spiritual problem as a result of his video game usage? If so, what was the nature of his problem, and how did it affect his faith?

4. In the end, the man was freed from his video game addiction. How did the man regain his freedom?

Where God builds His Church, the devil erects a chapel next to it.
—Martin Luther

CHAPTER

6

Spending the Day
with Spiritualists

*And no wonder, for even Satan disguises
himself as an angel of light. (2 Corinthians 11:14)*

I f you've ever driven past Birch Run on I-75 in Michigan, you may have
noticed the sign for the Birch Run Expo Center informing drivers of
upcoming events. This section of I-75 is often backed up for miles with
traffic in the summer when Michiganders are traveling north to their
cottages, so rarely does anyone miss the expo sign. Gun shows, hunting
shows, garden shows, and this week, the "Psychic Expo." Who goes to
those kinds of things anyway? Some of you may be surprised, and some of
you already know.

Psychic expos are becoming popular in the United Sates.

These events draw thousands of people who are searching for answers. Some of those who pass are frequent church attendees. Others who drive by include those who have felt let down by their church and decide to seek spiritual truth elsewhere. Some are followers of Wicca, Satanism, Buddhism, Hinduism, and just about every other religion you could name. One might expect that people who are drawn to this type of event are on the fringe of society. While this is true of some who attend, most of the people entering the doors of the expo center are just like you and your neighbors. Retirees, executives, factory workers, young couples, singles, and entire families including their children; the people who attend these events are no different than those you see visiting your neighborhood shopping mall.

Visiting a Psychic Expo

So what goes on inside of one of these expos? Maybe you have been to one before. Maybe you know what is about to be described in this chapter better than you would like to admit. Maybe you have thought such events and activities are good and God-pleasing or, at least, that they cause no harm. For those who have not participated in one of these spiritual expos, you will find a firsthand account of what goes on as you continue reading.

Attending the Psychic Expo is somewhat like attending a state or county fair. Throughout the day, the schedule is filled with various presentations. These presentations cover topics ranging from personal development to the power of spiritual beings, which the participants learn to call upon for assistance. What are some of the typical presentations from which one can choose? The Psychic Expo offered the following:

- Teaching Numerology
- Dowsing for the Health of It
- Free Clairvoyant Messages through Psychometry
- Tarot for Fun
- Communication with Angels
- Our Angels and Guides
- The Divine Female, How Mother God Has Been Silenced for 2,000 Years

While these seminars are well attended, they serve as distractions to help pass the time for those who have come for the expo's main attraction. Various new age vendors selling their books, crystals, and health and beauty products also divert the attendees. But looking around, it becomes obvious why the people are there. They wander from booth to booth signing their names in the appointment books laid out on the tables provided at the thresholds of various mediums' booths. The signs hanging over the booths describe what one will find within: angel readings, sound-wave therapy, hypnosis, pyramid energy, astrology, mystical art reading, aura readings, and clairvoyants. These are the real draw of those paying to enter the expo.

When the people are not wandering about in the expo center, watching the seminars, or shopping at the esoteric tables set up by the vendors, they take a seat in front of their chosen spiritual guide. There, they sit awaiting direction for their lost lives, healing from their diseases, freedom from the spirits that haunt them, or help for whatever other problems or concerns they may have carried in with them. Some of them have given up on their church and others have never entered a church in their lives.

Christianity in America continues to decline; it is almost impossible not to recognize this fact in our society. What many readers might fail to understand is that there are large numbers of people growing up in our country who have never heard the Gospel of Jesus. To them, churches are strange buildings they drive by as they make their way around town.

How do these nonbelievers view the people inside those churches? For many, the perception is negative. They view churchgoers as people who think themselves to be special. They view those gathered in the churches as hypocrites who worship on Sunday and live just like them the rest of the week. Some who have been apart from churches have been treated badly by church leaders and members.

Therefore, for some, the Psychic Expo, and the lost spirituality it panders, is their church. Here, they sit waiting for answers from demons dressed in the helpful and loving shells of mediums and alternate spiritual healers.

The Spiritualist Movement

What has been described in this chapter is probably not new to you. You are aware of these things, perhaps because you or someone close to you have attended similar events, or because you've heard about them in the media. One survey reports that 15 percent of people have been to a psychic

"If anyone is preaching to you a gospel contrary to the one you received, let him be accursed."—Galatians 1:8–9

or medium at some point in their life.[14] Yet one of the vendor tables at the Psychic Expo contained something that might come as a surprise to you. At first, it appeared to be just one more pamphlet among the many spread out on the various tables. But this pamphlet was different. The title read, "Good News: A Gathering of the Spirit." The pamphlet turned out to be a school catalog for a spiritualist seminary located in the state of Indiana.

A seminary is a place where people go to receive religious instruction in preparation for the ministry. Most Christian denominations have seminaries dedicated to the instruction of the Christian faith, after which its students are ordained and placed into public ministry. As it turns out, the spiritualism movement also uses seminaries to train and, in the end, ordain their students. This explains why all of the mediums and faith healers at the expo carried the title *Reverend*. Many of them were graduates of the spiritual seminary and had taken on the title.

The program provided by this particular "seminary" does not limit itself to adult students. It also offers an instructional option for children—a class entitled "Star Magic." For the meager price of sixty-five dollars, parents can send their children to this four-day camp. At this camp, the children will not only enjoy the activities found at any summer camp—arts and crafts, horseback riding, archery, and the like—but they will learn about the faith that they share with their families.

Beware of those who offer to take your children to their church summer camp! As our culture continues to seek the spiritual outside of the Christian Church, your neighbor may have something very different in mind for your children than you may expect. The same warning pertains to the various Vacation Bible Schools in your neighborhood. Parents can

---

14 Pew Research Center, "Eastern, New Age Beliefs Widespread: Many Americans Mix Multiple Faiths," www.pewforum.org/files/2009/12/multiplefaiths.pdf (accessed March 4, 2015).

no longer simply trust that what will be taught will be Christian. Even traditional churches are beginning to accept the teachings of the spiritualist movement. It is exactly in these settings that the spiritualist movement has become part of the broad American culture.

Martin Luther understood this problem already in the time of the Reformation. Luther once wrote, "Where God builds His Church, the devil erects a chapel next to it."[15] Luther's point was that the devil is always seeking to mimic the works of God. Speaking by the Spirit of God, St. Paul warned the Church, "But even if we or an angel from heaven should preach to you a gospel contrary to the one we preached to you, let him be accursed. As we have said before, so now I say again: If anyone is preaching to you a gospel contrary to the one you received, let him be accursed" (Galatians 1:8–9). The word *Gospel* means "Good News." In Scripture and Christian teaching, it is the Good News of the gracious gift of salvation through faith in Jesus Christ alone. Remember the title of the spiritualist seminary catalog? It was clear and to the point: "The Good News." But any spirituality that finds its origin or fulfillment outside of the means of Jesus' Word and Sacraments is a false spirituality, and hidden behind its facade is the devil and his demons.

---

15 Robert Kolb, *Luther and the Stories of God: Biblical Narratives as a Foundation for Christian Living* (Grand Rapids, MI: Baker Academic, 2012), 117.

Chapter 6 Study Questions

1. Have you ever attended a spiritual expo like the one mentioned in this chapter? If so, describe your experience. How did it compare to the events described above?

2. What, if any, dangers are there for Christians who attend an event like the one in this chapter?

3. Many unbelievers view Christians as hypocrites. Do you think this is a fair assumption? Explain your answer.

4. How many Americans have visited a medium or psychic in their lifetime? Does the answer surprise you? Why or why not?

5. What warning does Scripture give about seeking spiritual answers in places like the expo described above? (See Galatians 1:8–9.)

"Begone in the name of Jesus Christ."

CHAPTER

7

Don't Worry, Pastor, They Are Nice Ghosts

*Put on the whole armor of God, that you may be able to stand
against the schemes of the devil. (Ephesians 6:11)*

Most of what pastors know about their members comes from settings outside the church, such as conversation over a cup of coffee in their home, alongside the hospital bed, or, as in the following story, at a wedding reception. Like many pastors, the pastor in the following story, whom we will call Pastor Johnson, normally attends the wedding receptions of his members to say a prayer before the meal. This also provides an opportunity to get to know the church members and their extended family. Whenever a pastor spends time with the Lord's saints, he learns something new. But as you will see, the pastor in this story was not ready for what he was about to learn.

The story begins with a casual conversation between Pastor Johnson and a member of the church, whom we will call Kathy:

Kathy: *Pastor, sorry my husband and I missed church last week. We were out of town.*

Pastor Johnson: *No problem, I am sure you attend church somewhere else when you travel.*

Kathy: *Well . . . no, we did not make it to church this time.*

Pastor Johnson: *Okay, but you look like you want to tell me something.*

Kathy: *Ah . . . Pastor, I went to a paranormal conference this weekend.*

Pastor Johnson: *Why would you do that?*

Kathy: *You see, Pastor, we have ghosts in our home. They are very nice ghosts. They are the ghosts of two small children who died in a house fire more than one hundred years ago.*

Pastor Johnson: *We need to sit down and talk about this. Can you come see me in the office this week?*

Kathy: *Sure, I would like to do that. I tried to speak to one of our previous pastors about the situation, but he seemed to think there was something wrong with my family and me. Finally, he told me that if I wanted help I should probably go talk to a Roman Catholic priest.*

Pastor Johnson: *No, there is nothing wrong with you. Let's sit down and talk about these things next week.*

Kathy: *Thank you, Pastor. I have been looking for help for so long.*

According to one study, 47 percent of Americans report either having made contact with the dead or some other spiritual being that they described as a ghost. That number seems a bit high, but based on the openness of the spirituality of our time to mystical experiences (49 percent of Americans report having a mystical experience) these statistics may not be too far off.[16] It is very sad that members of Christian churches in America cannot get help from their pastors in areas that should be considered general pastoral care. Yet, this has been a problem for many years in our society. Rationalism and secularism have had devastating effects on the Christian Church and its pastors, and this remains a problem in our churches.

One of the most publicly recognized failures of the Lutheran Church comes from the case that inspired the movie *The Exorcist*. The movie was based on real events that took place in St. Louis, Missouri. What many people do not know is that before the Roman Catholic Church was charged with the exorcism, the Lutheran Church had already failed.

Why did the Lutherans fail and the Roman Catholics succeed in delivering the young boy (movie version was a girl) from the clutches of the devil? Darrell McCulley wrote and self-published a short book titled *The House Swept Clean: A Biblical Balanced Pattern for Diagnosis, Exorcism, and Pastoral Care of the Victims of Demonic Possession*,[17] in which he discusses the issue. While I disagree with many of the conclusions in McCulley's book, it is one of the few sources that deals with the situation of the St. Louis exorcism. In his book, McCulley seeks to understand why the Lutheran pastors involved with the exorcism failed to help the young man who was demon possessed. To make a long story short, they simply lacked the experience and resources to deal with the topic of the demonic. In fact, many of the pastors didn't believe in the possibility of demonic possession. By the time they recognized what was happening, they had lost the child to the Roman Catholic Church.

How many other people have suffered under the power of the devil because Christian clergy have failed to proclaim the freedom of Jesus who breaks the bonds of Satan? Too many to count, I would expect. Kathy was one of those who had been let down by her pastor.

---

16 Pew Research Center, "Eastern, New Age Beliefs Widespread: Many Americans Mix Multiple Faiths," www.pewforum.org/files/2009/12/multiplefaiths.pdf (accessed March 4, 2015).

17 St. Louis: Darrell A. McCulley, 2002. For those who are looking for a copy of this book, it is no longer in print, but some copies of the PDF can still be found.

When Kathy visited Pastor Johnson in his office, he asked her, "Why did you go to the paranormal conference?" Kathy replied, "Because our previous pastor would not help me, and I did not want to go to the Roman Catholic priest, so it was the only other option I could think of."

Pastor Johnson was distressed that a member of his church would seek council in such a non-Christian setting. As he struggled to understand the family's circumstances, he asked, "So what did you learn at the paranormal conference?" Kathy's response surprised him:

> *Pastor, I learned that these ghosts are good ghosts and that I should not be afraid of them. All I have to do is treat them nicely and ignore some of the antics, and everything will be okay. So now when we see the two little children, we try to make contact with them. When they pull the sheets off the bed, we laugh. When they make noises, we just say, "There go the kids again."*

Pastor Johnson recognized that something in Kathy's voice still did not sound right. After some additional conversation, Kathy revealed that sometimes the family was truly afraid for their safety. Pastor Johnson explained to Kathy that there were no such things as ghosts. If there was anything truly going on in her house, it was not a ghost that was causing these problems. If the events Kathy was describing were real, they must be understood as demonic in nature. Pastor Johnson suspected that Kathy was already aware of this, and that she had been trying to tell herself a lie because the truth was too terrifying for her to accept.

Pastor Johnson and Kathy read through a few passages in the New Testament, including Hebrews 9:27–28, "Just as it is appointed for man to die once, and after that comes judgment, so Christ, having been offered once to bear the sins of many, will appear a second time, not to deal with sin but to save those who are eagerly waiting for Him" and Philippians 1:23, "I am hard pressed between the two. My desire is to depart and be with Christ, for that is far better." Soon, Kathy was convinced that the spirits her family saw were not children nor ghosts but, in fact, demons. The other possibility could have been that Kathy and her family suffered from mental illness or an overactive imagination, but both of these things were discounted because every member of the family reported seeing and hearing these things when they were gathered in the same room.

Now that Kathy agreed that the problem was demonic in nature, Pastor Johnson suggested that they should move forward and deal with the problem once and for all. He explained to the family that in such cases the next step would be a house blessing, which, as he explained to them, is actually another name for an exorcism. They agreed and set the date for the exorcism.

As Pastor Johnson arrived at the old farmhouse, Kathy and her husband, Earl, met him at the door. "Okay, Pastor, where do we start?" Pastor Johnson asked for a tour of the house. He wanted to know where they were seeing most of the spirits. They proceeded room by room. In each room, he read various Scripture passages and prayed prayers that declared the lordship of Jesus and requested peace to return in Jesus' name. In the most problematic areas of the house, he spoke the words, "Begone in the name of Jesus Christ."

Most people who hear this story have been so conditioned by popular ghost stories that they expect a dramatic response. The movies would have us believe that each time Pastor Johnson spoke, the house shook and voices cried out. No, that wasn't the case. Nor, in most instances, is it ever the case. The whole event was nothing special—no spirits, no ghost, no noises, absolutely nothing. So how did Pastor Johnson know the exorcism worked? Because the family who had been stricken with fear for more than forty years has not had a single strange or spiritual encounter with the demons since the day of the exorcism. Five years after the incident, the house remains quiet and peaceful. Too often, we forget where our real help lies, but Jesus remains the defeater of sin, death, and the devil. There is safety

There is safety in knowing that even though he is a trickster, Satan and his demons are powerless in Jesus' presence.

in the name of Jesus. There is safety in knowing that even though he is a trickster, Satan and his demons are powerless in Jesus' presence. As you continue to read through the pages of this book, this truth will become more evident.

Chapter 7 Study Questions

1. According to the survey quoted in this chapter, what percentage of Americans report seeing a ghost or communicating with the dead? What are your thoughts about this statistic? Did the percentage seem high to you? Why or why not?

2. Why did the Christian family in this story seek out the assistance of the paranormal investigators?

3. Do ghosts exist? What Scripture passages help answer this question?

They saw an expressionless look as if the child was in a deep trance.

CHAPTER 8

There Is Something Wrong with the Children

The light is among you for a little while longer. Walk while you have the light, lest darkness overtake you. (John 12:35)

Since writing my first book, I have received numerous emails and phone calls from pastors seeking advice regarding the spiritual problems of their members. As a result, I have heard more stories than I can provide in the pages of this book. The story you are about to read is one of the more troubling stories I have heard. I include it here to help readers understand some of the realities their pastors deal with on an ongoing basis but would rarely discuss. Due to confidentiality, none of the actual names or places are disclosed.

Baptism, Exorcism, and Release

"I have a problem with some members of my church." This is how the phone call began as Pastor Smith reached out for help from one of his brother pastors. He was extremely worried about some young children that were new to his church. One of the families in his congregation had purchased a new home in the area while at the same time adopting two children, a five-year-old boy, whom we will call Jimmy, and a four-year-old girl, whom we will call Julie. The family had also recently added to their family with the birth of a new baby. They went from having no children to having three children in a short time. Such a change would be difficult for any family to adjust to. I expect that the family knew this as they entered into the situation, but there was no way they could be ready for what was about to happen to them and their children. They had hoped to start a new life, and this was just the beginning. Still, it was not the beginning they expected.

Pastor Smith explained the background of the problem:

> Immediately upon moving in, the family began to experience a host of demonic activity ranging from footsteps, sounds of pouring rain when it wasn't raining, sounds of doors opening and closing, physical manifestations—bites and feelings of someone climbing into bed, sightings of "ghosts," personality changes in members of the household. The father confessed to thoughts of murder, suicide, and divorce and said that he was "too evil to come to church."

Most unnerving to the parents was the strange activity that was now appearing in the adopted children. Typical childish behaviors turned into something far different.

The parents started to notice four-year-old Julie talking to what she believed to be an imaginary friend. They did not believe that this was too big of a deal because at that age many children pretend to have invisible friends. The real problem came with Jimmy, the five-year-old boy. Almost nightly, Jimmy was found walking around the house in a daze. Moreover, when he awoke in the morning, he could not remember his actions from the previous night. Once again, these things happen. I am sure anyone with young children has experienced such activity. There is nothing strange about some occasional sleepwalking. At least, that's what the parents had told themselves until the one night when everything changed.

As the new parents lay asleep in bed, they awoke to the sound of their newborn infant screaming. The parents proceeded down the hallway, as they no doubt had done many times before. The walk down the hallway was a short one taking only a few moments. As the parents tiredly approached the child's bedroom, they noticed the light in the room was lighting up the hallway. Both of them remembered the light being off when they went to bed that night. The child was an infant, so they knew the child could not have turned on the light. Thinking that one of them must have left the light on before going to bed, they entered the room to comfort the crying child.

As they opened the partially closed door, the terror they were about to experience was unimaginable. There, standing in front of their newborn child, was Jimmy. Understandably, this in itself was not to be unexpected given the child's previous activities. Nevertheless, when the parents entered the room, they could not believe what they saw. Jimmy was standing in front of the crib rubbing his feces all over their baby's face and in his mouth. They grabbed Jimmy and pulled him away from the baby. As they looked into his eyes, they saw an expressionless look as if the child was in a deep trance. When Jimmy regained his consciousness, he claimed to have no memory of what he had done to the baby.

The parents were at a loss as to what to do. When morning came, they knew they had to contact their pastor for help. They explained to Pastor Smith all the previous events, including the strange occurrences in the home and the unnerving actions of their adopted children. It was at this point that Pastor Smith contacted another pastor for assistance. It is always good for pastors to recognize they are not alone in their work. The Lord provides varying gifts to pastors and expects them to work together.

Where does a pastor begin when faced with such problems? A well-catechized reader should already recognize the answer. The children were not baptized. Pastor Smith had been talking to the parents about the importance of Baptism for their adopted children since they had entered the family's house. But the parents' excuse was the same as many parents of young children. They claimed to be too busy. They said the renovations to their home were behind, and they wanted it to be complete before having the extended family visit for such an event. While previously there seemed no reason to rush into anything, now the parents changed their minds and wanted the children baptized as soon as possible. Pastor Smith agreed to baptize the children and requested that the family invite him and the pastor he had called for assistance over for a house blessing as well.

Baptism and exorcism have always been historically connected. Such a statement may seem strange. Traditionally, Baptism is understood to be the action of God that brings faith to the individual. There are two texts that show the connection between Baptism and exorcism. The first text comes from the Gospel of John:

> [Jesus said,] "Now is the judgment of this world; now will the ruler of this world be cast out. And I, when I am lifted up from the earth, will draw all people to myself." He said this to show by what kind of death He was going to die. So the crowd answered Him, "We have heard from the Law that the Christ remains forever. How can you say that the Son of Man must be lifted up? Who is this Son of Man?" So Jesus said to them, "The light is among you for a little while longer. Walk while you have the light, lest darkness overtake you. The one who walks in the darkness does not know where he is going. While you have the light, believe in the light, that you may become sons of light." When Jesus had said these things, He departed and hid Himself from them. Though He had done so many signs before them, they still did not believe in Him. (12:31–37)

In this text, Jesus points to His own death upon the cross as an act of exorcism.[18] This exorcism is a culmination of all the other exorcisms found within the New Testament Scriptures. It is the ultimate picture of the spiritual battle being waged upon the earth. At the cross, Jesus will cast out (exorcize) Satan. The accuser of men will lose his power because all sin is exonerated in Jesus' death. The prince of this world is cast off his throne by the One who dies in the place of all humanity upon the cross. When this text is added to our next text, its connection to Baptism will become clearer.

One of the most vivid New Testament texts concerning Baptism comes from the writings of St. Paul in Romans 6. Paul writes:

> Do you not know that all of us who have been baptized into Christ Jesus were baptized into His death? We were buried therefore with Him by Baptism into death, in order that, just as Christ was raised from the dead by the glory of the Father, we too might walk in newness of life. (vv. 3–4)

While St. John connects exorcism with the crucifixion, St. Paul links the exorcistic work of the crucifixion to Baptism. In Baptism, the individual is connected to Jesus' crucifixion and resurrection, thereby receiving freedom from the devil and his demons.

In Romans 6:13–14, Paul concludes:

> Do not present your members to sin as instruments for unrighteousness, but present yourselves to God as those who have been brought from death to life, and your members to God as instruments for righteousness. For sin will have no dominion over you, since you are not under law but under grace.

---

18 Marianne Meyer Thompson, *The Incarnate Word: Perspectives on Jesus in the Fourth Gospel* (Peabody, MA: Hendrickson Publishers, 1993), 94.

Sin, which includes the author of sin, Satan, "will have no dominion over you." There is freedom in Baptism, because through Baptism one is connected to the freedom provided in the crucifixion and resurrection of Jesus. For the spiritually oppressed, the connection between Baptism and exorcism cannot be overstated. Baptism is not magic. It is not a spell of protection but the promise of Jesus' presence and forgiveness. By extension, the house blessing has nothing to do with spiritual words or rites but with the presence of Jesus, who connects Himself by the power of the Holy Spirit to His Word.

The Lutheran Church has retained the rite of a house blessing. Sometimes the rite is referred to as the dedication of a dwelling. Whatever nomenclature one chooses does not matter. At the heart of these forms of blessings lies an exorcistic prayer. Pastor Smith knew that both Baptism and an exorcism of the house should take place as soon as possible.

The date for both the Baptism and the house blessing was set for the following week. At Pastor Smith's suggestion, the parents would refrain from telling the children what was about to take place in the home to avoid any added fear they might experience if they were aware that an exorcism was going to take place in their home.

As the day approached, things got worse. Jimmy developed a terrible fear of water. Julie began acting violently toward the boy. The day before the Baptism, both of the children covered themselves in dog feces. When asked why they did this, Jimmy answered, "I don't want to get clean." Nevertheless, both of the children were in church for the service.

Jimmy and Julie were baptized on the Feast of the Ascension of Our Lord. Like many Lutheran churches, this church had a special midweek service to celebrate the ascension. On this evening, the two children who had been tormented received the words, "I baptize you in the name of the Father and of the Son and of the Holy Spirit."

As the water of life was poured out over their heads, a transformation was taking place. These young children were being connected to Jesus' crucifixion and resurrection. They were being freed from sin, death, and the devil. Following their Baptisms, some of the family members took the children out to celebrate, with the promise of ice cream for dessert. The real reason for the celebration was to give Pastor Smith and his fellow pastor time to return to the children's home and perform the house blessing without them being present.

As the pastors traveled, Pastor Smith told his brother pastor of a conversation he had with the father moments before the Baptism. The father said that as he was preparing to leave his house for the church, the chandelier fell from the ceiling, just missing his head. Could this simply be a coincidence? Sure, but it did make the pastors a bit nervous—especially considering the events of the past few days.

Over the years, I have spoken with pastors who try to avoid anything connected with exorcism. I suspect that one of the problems is lack of formal training in dealing with something like exorcism. Likewise, neither of these pastors was sure what might be coming their way. Still, they knew that they were called to faithfully speak the Word of peace and forgiveness. These pastors were going to do what pastors are called to do.

Risky Business

Many vocations carry a certain amount of exposure to risky situations. Police officers frequently encounter danger, as do firemen, soldiers, medical personnel, and first responders. However, within the Western world, being a pastor does not usually come with too many risks. This may be another reason why Western pastors experience anxiety when they are called to perform an exorcism. However, many other areas of the world require their pastors to operate in the midst of constant danger. These pastors have related stories of how the local witch doctors would seek to kill them for preaching the Gospel and disturbing the income they receive. Thankfully, Pastor Smith and his fellow pastor did not need to worry about such outward aggression.

The home where the exorcism was to take place was easy to spot as the pastors turned down the residential street. It was a beautiful nine-teenth-century dwelling that had been completely restored. After parking in front of the house, the pastors waited for the parents to arrive, and then the four adults entered the house together. Pastor Smith explained to the parents the nature of the rite that he would be performing in the home. Although there are various forms of house-blessing rites available for pastors to use, few of them are explicitly exorcisms. This is most likely due to the Western world's Rationalistic worldview. Normally, such house blessings only carry one short exorcistic prayer buried in the many prayers and Scripture readings. But rather than using the short rite of blessing, Pastor Smith took what he believed to be the most helpful aspects of the various rites and combined them.

Pastor Smith and his colleague began moving from room to room reading various Scripture passages and praying the exorcistic prayers. In the areas where the family noticed the majority of the problems, they paused and spoke the words, "Begone in the name of Jesus Christ." One of the more eerie sections of the home was the basement. That is where Jimmy and Julie had been sleeping following the terrible situation that occurred between the infant and the boy. In each section of the basement, the pastors took extra time to pray. Were there any demonic signs? Were the spirits seeking to communicate? Were items flying around the room? No, nothing out of the ordinary was seen or heard. The only sounds came from the pastors as they went from room to room praying the Lord's Prayer and singing traditional Christian hymns.

There was one room left to bless. As they entered the living room, they concluded the exorcism with the hymn "A Mighty Fortress Is Our God." This is a hymn written by Martin Luther, who was no stranger to the work of the devil and his demons. If one were to look closely at both the Lord's Prayer and this hymn, one would notice that both are exorcistic in nature. The Lord's Prayer requests that God would deliver us from evil. The original Greek can also be translated, "Deliver us from the evil one." The hymn also speaks of the Word of God undoing the work of the evil one. The second part of stanza 3 states, "This world's prince may still Scowl fierce as he will. He can harm us none. He's judged; the deed is done; One little word can fell him."[19]

Luther recognized that Jesus is the only exorcist and that only Jesus can dislodge Satan and his devils. Both the Lord's Prayer and the hymn declare this truth as they both recognize the ongoing work of Satan, while at the same time recognizing that he is a defeated foe who has no power over the children of God. As they concluded the prayers, Pastor Smith thought he noticed something move past them by the entryway, but he could not be sure. Nevertheless, it really did not matter. The pastors were not there as paranormal investigators looking to gather data or proof of the paranormal. They were simply speaking the words of their Savior. Indeed, it is best to ignore any strange activity that occurs while performing an exorcism. Such activity can distract the pastor, preventing him from speaking in the stead of Jesus. If the pastor, even for a moment, looks to his own devices in these situations, he is opening himself up to danger. This is true in any function that the pastor performs in his Office, whether he is performing a house blessing, performing an exorcism, preaching, or presiding over the Sacraments. In each of these cases, the pastor is acting in the stead of Jesus without any power or worthiness in himself. Such knowledge is freeing for the pastor when he is charged to serve in difficult situations. Indeed, this knowledge is freeing for all Christians when they realize that Jesus is present for them through the pastoral care they receive. The family would need ongoing pastoral care. The house exorcism was not a magical fix. Through the words spoken in their home, Jesus was present, but ongoing catechesis was necessary. Many in our culture might question the need for pastoral care and weekly church attendance; therefore, this is a good place to discuss these things in more detail.

In his book *Mission from the Cross*, Dr. Klaus Detlev Schulz provides a definition of the Church, connecting it with Baptism and Jesus' crucifixion. Schulz writes:

---

19 *LSB* 656.

The visible signs of the Church, around which believers gather, form the spiritual life of a Christian community. Particularly in the context of a dominant heathen culture, the Sacraments ultimately serve as a barricade against the perpetual onslaught of non-Christian elements on the believers. The gifts that began to shape the life of the community in Baptism continue to strengthen the fellowship through the Sacrament of the Altar. The Church is a sacramental community living in alien and hostile situations, and the Sacrament of the Lord's Supper affirms her as that. The Church of Christ thus lives in and from the Sacraments.[20]

Jesus is present through His Word and Sacraments. Through these gifts, He provides life, forgiveness, healing, and protection from the evil one. Jesus is the only exorcist. Humanity cannot defeat Satan or his demons by the use of mere words or rituals. Through the gifts of Holy Baptism and the Lord's Supper, the power of Jesus' Word is attached to the elements of water, bread, and wine, therefore connecting Jesus to the individual. A similar promise of the forgiveness of sins is attached to the Rite of Confession and Absolution. Where there is the forgiveness of sins, Satan has lost his stronghold, and peace is found (Acts 26:17–18).

Although the exorcism of the home and the Baptism of the children brought peace to the young family, their only hope for an ongoing peace was found in the protection of Jesus. Consider again Jesus' words regarding what happens during an exorcism:

> When the unclean spirit has gone out of a person, it passes through waterless places seeking rest, but finds none. Then it says, "I will return to my house from which I came." And when it comes, it finds the house empty, swept, and put in order. Then it goes and brings with it seven other spirits more

---

20 Klaus Detlev Schulz, *Mission from the Cross: The Lutheran Theology of Mission* (St. Louis: Concordia, 2009), 206.

AFRAID

evil than itself, and they enter and dwell there, and the last state of that person is worse than the first." (Matthew 12:43–45; cf. Luke 11:24–26)

This text is significant because it provides insight into the reality of demon possession and exorcism. Without the presence of the Holy Spirit, a person, even after receiving release and forgiveness, can experience greater difficulties if not continually connected to his or her Savior. Ongoing pastoral care, church attendance, and personal devotion and prayer all provide protection from the assaults of the evil one. Still, the focus must always be on Jesus and never upon personal piety or power.

After a while, the demonic activity in the family's home decreased, and in the end, it finally disappeared. At first, the family was surprised that the exorcism did not work immediately, but through continual pastoral care they came to understand that the performance of an exorcism does not guarantee immediate removal of an evil spirit. In this case, things improved, but over the next few months additional exorcisms were required.

Jesus warns His apostles that they should not expect the demons to go willingly. When His disciples had similar concerns, He said, "This kind cannot be driven out by anything but prayer" (see Mark 9:14–29). The things mentioned here include the evil spirits who are under the control of God. They must depart when He requires them to do so. When Christians pray for God's protection and speak boldly the Word of God, thus forcing the devils to tremble, this trembling is not a result of our words but the presence of Jesus, who connects Himself to the Word. And it is the duty of the pastor to speak in the stead of Jesus. Yet, Satan and his demons sometimes bring problems upon the pastors who confront them. Such was the case with Jimmy and Julie's pastor.

On the night of the exorcism, Pastor Smith's son began experiencing night terrors. A night terror occurs when someone awakes from sleeping but is unable to move. Many times, people afflicted by night terrors report a dark presence in the room that physically attacks them while they remain defenseless. How did Pastor Smith handle this attack upon his son? He performed a house blessing on his own home. As a result of the exorcism, his son's night terrors immediately ceased. Many pastors avoid exorcisms and home blessings because they worry about bringing spiritual danger upon their own families. Yet, as this story demonstrates, Satan is weak and Jesus easily expels him; therefore, fear should not prevent pastors from fulfilling their calling. Daily, each of God's children face spiritual warfare. There is no way to avoid such things as a Christian. The only difference is the intensity of the attack. In fact, demonic spirits, like the ones described in this book, are easier to recognize and dispatch than the more subtle common spiritual attacks that all Christians experience.

Where It All Started

Each person has one or more specific sins that plague him or her. Many times, these sins are hidden from even one's closest friends and family. These are the recurring sinful thoughts that seem to come to us from out of nowhere. Sometimes we act on these sinful desires and sometimes not, but the fact remains, these are recurring struggles, spiritual battles, which we face all the time. It would be wrong to suggest that the sinful thoughts and tendencies we endure are all satanic attacks waged upon us by the devil. Original sin has corrupted us so that apart from Jesus all people are slaves to sins. As a result, we are easily coaxed into following the old man within us.

While it is not within the scope of this book to provide a lengthy discussion of original sin and its consequences on humanity, a short explanation is necessary. The Epistle to the Romans provides a helpful introduction to the old man/new man paradox. In Romans 5:12–19, St. Paul presents the answer to our sin in his description of the new Adam, which is Jesus, and the old Adam, the historical figure Adam, as found in the Book of Genesis. Jesus entered the world to set right the sin of Adam that continues to cling to his offspring. In chapter 7 of Romans, Paul demonstrates that our transformation from the old man to the new man takes place in

Holy Baptism. In Baptism, the old man within us dies, or, as Luther says, he is drowned. Out of that same water, a new man rises with Christ. Yet even though the old man of sin has been killed, he has not completely lost his grip upon us. Many Christian denominations refuse to accept that Paul could be speaking of himself as a Christian. They attempt to read Romans 7 as Paul describing his earlier life as an unbeliever. However, Paul's theology is clear: even after receiving the new man of faith, his old man of sin remains behind. To be sure, Paul recognizes that the old man has a wounded nature in the Christian, but wounded or not, the old man is quite capable of causing the Christian to return to his previous sinful ways. This transformation from old man to new man is also demonstrated in Ephesians 2, in which Paul states that apart from the gift of Jesus all men are spiritually dead, following the desires of their sin and the devil (vv. 1–10).

While the Christian is a new creation, the old Adam within him is in allegiance to Satan and his evil forces. The struggle between following the will of God and the will of the devil is a constant spiritual battle that will continue until the day of the Christian's death. This struggle can occur in subtle attacks, or it can lead the Christian into dangers far worse than seeing a demon or being attacked by spiritual forces at home. Still, in whatever form these spiritual attacks come, the cure is the same. The answer is Jesus, and His medicine is His Word and Sacraments. Whenever we speak about the Word and Sacraments as medicine or as weapons and shields (Ephesians 6:10–18), we also need to be reminded why they are effective against the assaults of the devil and our own sin. The effectiveness of the Word and the Sacraments is due to their connection with the person of Jesus. He is our protector and the answer for all sin—whether the sin of the flesh or the author of sin and his demons. In Jesus, we have the victory over sin, death, and the devil.

Chapter 8 Study Questions

1. Why do some pastors avoid the topic of exorcism?

2. Why did Pastor Smith seek the assistance of a brother pastor before assisting the family in the story?

3. What role did Baptism play in this story?

4. Where might one find the connection between exorcism and the crucifixion in John's Gospel?

5. How are Baptism, exorcism, the crucifixion, and the resurrection of Jesus connected?

6. What does the liturgical rite of a house blessing involve? Ask your pastor to review the rite with you.

7. Read Matthew 12:43–45 and Luke 11:26. What do these verses teach us about demon possession and the activities of demons?

8. Is the personal holiness or piety of a person a factor in his or her ability to drive an evil spirit from a house? Explain your answer.

9. Why are Christian devotions an important part of the Christian life? Why are they especially important to the Christian who is facing a spiritual struggle like the one described in this chapter?

Satan and his demons are powerless in Jesus' presence.

CHAPTER

9

WHAT DOES AN EXORCISM LOOK LIKE?

This kind cannot be driven out by anything but prayer.
(Mark 9:29)

" Pastor, I heard you on the radio speaking about your book. Can you help me?" This is how the phone conversation began. A woman from a Lutheran congregation, we will call her Janice, had heard me speaking on the topic of demon possession and exorcism as a guest on a popular nationwide radio program. As a result of hearing the broadcast, the woman purchased a copy of my book, *I Am Not Afraid*, and began reading it.

It was not just curiosity that compelled Janice to read the book. She had a problem, and she was looking for answers. Her problem was her brother Randy. Randy had been an organist for his church. He had been playing the hymns and the liturgy at his church for years, but Randy had a secret. During his years of active service to the church, Randy had also been practicing witchcraft. The form of witchcraft he was involved in sought to place curses on people by using the "evil eye." The evil eye is a form of curse that is placed on someone by looking at them with evil intent.

Many folk religions believe in the evil eye. It can be found in several cultures including Latin America and the Middle East.[21] We don't know for sure if the evil eye is real, but many millions of people in the world continue to believe that it is and that it is something that can be used to harm one's neighbor. While some people believe that the power of the evil eye resides within the individual who uses it, many Christians would understand the power of the evil eye to come from demons, which at the request of the sender, can attack an individual. Many voodoo practitioners also believe that the curses they cast are carried out by the work of the spirits.[22]

Randy had lived this lifestyle for many years until he finally suffered a nervous breakdown. Janice reported that her brother had begun to see spirits, and sometimes they would attack him. The attacks were not physical, but instead they were of a more threatening nature. The spirits would tell Randy that he was going to be held accountable to God for the evil he had done. The spirits warned him that others would soon learn of his curses, and he would be taken to prison. In mental health terms, we would generally speak of such notions as psychotic hallucinations or schizophrenia.[23] While medical treatment should always be sought in such circumstances, many people who have experienced such symptoms have found relief through Christian prayers and exorcism.

As Janice read the book, she noticed that the stories I related were similar to her brother's story. If prayer and exorcism could help those people, Janice thought that an exorcism might also provide relief for Randy.

---

21 For more information on the evil eye in an Islamic culture, see Bill Musk, *The Unseen Face of Islam: Sharing the Gospel with Ordinary Muslims at Street Level* (Grand Rapids, MI: Monarch Books, 2004), 242–44.

22 I have spoken to some highly acclaimed voodoo priests in Haiti on the subject of curses. All of them agreed that curses can only be placed upon nonfaithful Christians and unbelievers. The voodoo priests were very clear that they don't even attempt to curse Christians, because they recognize that the God who protects us is greater than any of their gods.

23 See "Schizophrenia Spectrum and Other Psychotic Disorders" in *Diagnostic and Statistical Manual of Mental Disorders: DSM-5* (Washington DC: American Psychiatric Association, 2013), 115.

Janice asked, "Can you please help my brother?" I asked her to describe her brother's condition. My questions included the following:

1. Does your brother belong to a church?

2. Does his pastor know about these problems?

3. Has your brother received medical help?

The answers to these questions are necessary to determine the spiritual state of the individual. As it turned out, Randy had not attended church for a number of years due to his mental state. Nevertheless, his own pastor had been faithfully visiting him, bringing the Word of God and the Sacraments to his home. The problem was that Randy's pastor was not aware of his previous exposure to the occult. He was a new pastor who had just begun serving the church. While the pastor knew that Randy had mental issues and had been under the care of both mental health professionals and Christian counselors, he knew nothing of Randy's hidden spiritual problems. The doctors had prescribed SSRIs (selective serotonin reuptake inhibitors) for the depression and anxiety problems that Randy was experiencing, as well as Risperidone for schizophrenia. Neither of the medications provided Randy with relief. Both of these medications, along with the medical history provided by his sister, pointed toward anxiety disorders, depression, and schizophrenia. For many pastors in America, this would be enough to dissuade them from looking for spiritual answers. Yet, I maintain that leaving such cases in the hands of medicine alone is a failure to perform one's pastoral duties. Moreover, none of the medications, nor the counseling, seemed to be providing relief to the tormented man's soul.

Luther on Demonical Possession and Satan

Before continuing with the story, we must first answer a question: Can a Christian be demon possessed? While many Christians provide compelling arguments why this should not be possible, the history of the Church says otherwise. On this question, I follow Martin Luther and other Christian leaders who hold that a Christian can be oppressed by demons. Moreover, under exceedingly rare conditions Christians can also be physically possessed.

Luther is characterized (often by his detractors) as a man who found the devil everywhere. Luther fully accepted that Satan remains active in the world. He understood the devil to be an adversary who was always causing both spiritual and physical harm to humanity. He understood very well that some of the afflictions presented to him for counsel had spiritual causes while others had physical causes, and sometimes both may be encountered simultaneously.[24]

DEMONIC POSSESSION

In one such case, Luther offered counsel to Pastor Bernard Wurzelmann regarding a situation in which a woman was possessed by the devil:

> The first thing you and your congregation ought to do is this: pray fervently and oppose Satan with your faith, no matter how stubbornly he resists. About ten years ago, we had an experience in this neighborhood with a very wicked demon, but we succeeded in subduing him by perseverance and by unceasing prayer and unquestioning faith. The same will happen among you if you continue in Christ's name to despise that derisive and arrogant spirit and do not cease praying. By this means I have restrained many similar spirits in different places, for the prayers of the Church prevail at last.[25]

Luther advised Pastor Wurzelmann that the Church and prayer were the primary ways to deal with this case of possession. The Church is the place where the faithful gather around the Word of Jesus and the Holy Sacraments. Through these means, Jesus has promised to be present as a loving protector who pours out His forgiveness upon our sin-ridden bodies and souls. In the presence of Jesus, Satan cannot stand. Moreover, it is in the Divine Service of the Church where we meet as the people of God with our combined petitions. We pray, "Our Father . . . " as the collective body of Christ on this earth, and Jesus promises to hear and answer our prayers.

---

24 Theodore G. Tappert, ed., *Luther: Letters of Spiritual Counsel* (New York: Westminster John Knox Press, 2006), 18.

25 Tappert, *Luther*, 42.

AFRAID

SATAN, AND PHYSICAL AND MENTAL DISEASE

In another instance, Luther dealt with the differences between physical causes and demonic causes of disease. Often, the Church has simply turned cases of mental disorders and other afflictions over to the medical establishment without even considering that the affliction is demonically imposed. No doubt, such talk may cause many who read this to feel a bit uncomfortable. You might be thinking, "This is just not the way Lutherans talk." Well, if this describes you, then just wait: this is exactly the way Luther addressed the problem in his counsel to Anthony Lauterbach:

> Physicians observe only the natural causes of illness and try to counteract these by means of their remedies. They do well to do this. But they do not understand that Satan is sometimes the instigator of the material cause of the disease; he can alter the causes and diseases at once, and he can turn a fever into chills and health into illness. To deal with Satan there must be a higher medicine, namely, faith and prayer.[26]

Science and natural causes should not be our answer for every affliction. Physicians are gifts of God and workers of His healing, but many times there are spiritual causes behind physical problems. We would do well to remember this scriptural teaching when dealing with the sick and afflicted.

DEMONIC SUICIDE

If the way Luther talked about demonic possession causes you discomfort, his counsel to a widow who had recently lost her husband to suicide may be even more difficult to accept. Christians struggle over the salvation of those who inflict injury and death upon themselves. While many times suicide is the result of chemical changes in the brain that can be treated by modern medicine, sometimes there seems to be no indication of these things. At other times, suicide might be the ultimate act of unbelief; such acts end in condemnation by God.

---

26 Tappert, *Luther*, 46.

However, Luther was ahead of his time in recognizing another cause of suicide that many within our time have passed over. On many occasions, individuals who commit suicide do not freely choose to do so but may be driven to suicide by the devil, the world, and their own sinful nature. Therefore, Luther comforted the widow as he wrote:

> That your husband inflicted injury upon himself may be explained by the devil's power over our members. He may have directed your husband's hand even against his will. For if your husband had done what he did of his own free will, he would surely not have come to himself and turned to Christ with such a confession of faith. How often the devil breaks arms, legs, backs, and all members! He can be master of the body and its members against our will.[27]

Luther understood the suicidal man to be a Christian and accepted the idea that Christians may be subject to possession by demons. In stating that Satan directed the hand of the man, it could be that Satan planted the thought or suggestion into the man's mind to kill himself. But it could just as well mean that Satan did the deed through literally possessing the man's hands. Should not the Church at least consider such things? How many deaths could be prevented by recognizing the work of Satan and casting it away by the name of Jesus? I will leave this for you to consider as we return to Janice and her brother Randy.

The Liturgy as Exorcism

"So where do we go from here?" While the reader may be asking this question, this question was absolutely on my mind as I considered Janice's call for help. Randy was a member of another church. That meant that God had assigned him to the care of a particular pastor. It would be inappropriate for me to go any further without speaking to the pastor who was called to provide for Randy's spiritual care. I assured Janice that while

---

27 Tappert, *Luther*, 59.

I would do anything I could to help, I would only do so if Randy's pastor requested my help. I also insisted that Randy agree that whatever he and I talked about, including the sins discussed in confession, I could also share with his own pastor.

At first, this request might seem strange. A confession of sins must remain confidential and should be forgotten as soon as it is absolved. Martin Luther reminded the Church that it is the Lord who hears the confession, but He uses the ears and the mouth of the pastor in the confessional setting.[28] The pastor simply hears the confession on behalf of Jesus, and the forgiveness that the pastor speaks is Jesus' forgiveness, not the pastor's. Yet, in this case it was necessary for Randy's pastor to be informed of the circumstances so that he could continue to provide for Randy's spiritual care.

The next day, Randy's pastor called and said, "I just don't know how to help Randy." The pastor had been faithfully visiting Randy for many months without knowing of Randy's previous involvement with the occult. Randy's pastor assured me that he was now aware of the situation, and gave his permission for me to do anything I thought was necessary to help the troubled man. After some additional conversation, it was decided that Randy would visit me so that I could perform an exorcism. The date was set for the following Sunday.

That Sunday, a small car pulled into the parking lot, and Janice and Randy exited their car and began to walk toward the church. Janice was nicely dressed and wore a crucifix necklace. Randy had a disheveled appearance with a crooked grin that seemed to be engraved on his face. It was apparent he was anxious about the meeting. I led them directly into the church's sanctuary. A chair had been set up next to the baptismal font located in the front of the church. Randy sat down, and I began with Confession and Absolution. Randy confessed his sin of seeking power from the demons. He also confessed that he had cast curses upon others. Randy

---

28 Martin Luther, *What Luther Says: A Practical In-Home Anthology for the Active Christian*, compiled by Ewald M. Plass (St. Louis: Concordia, 1986), §§ 980–81, 1831.

related that he had tried to confess these sins to another pastor once before. But as Randy confessed his sin of witchcraft to that pastor, the pastor had responded by laughing at him. He then told Randy that he must be making these things up and that he could not help Randy "if he was going to be telling such fanciful stories." From that day on, Randy refused to confess his sins to a pastor again—that is, until now. Following his confession, Randy received the sweet words of the Gospel, "I forgive you all your sins in the name of the Father and of the Son and of the Holy Spirit."

In the speaking of the Gospel, Satan and his demons are forced to retreat with their lying words of condemnation. They had told this man for years that his sin could not be forgiven and that the pastors would not understand. Therefore, he should just give up and die. Now, finally, their words were shown to be lies. Randy, who had lived in the torment of his sins for so long, now heard a sure, objective word from God, "You are forgiven."

As was stated earlier, the word *exorcism* comes from the Greek word *ekballō*, which means "to cast out." The Rite of Confession and Absolution does just that. Satan and sin are cast out with the words of the Gospel. The apostle John says it best when he writes, "The reason the Son of God appeared was to destroy the works of the devil" (1 John 3:8). The works of the devil are cast away in the work of Jesus. Holy Absolution is the work of Jesus, and where the light of Jesus stands, evil must flee. This is not how Hollywood or even how many churches would view exorcism, but we are not speaking here of the things of the world. We speak only of the things of God.

The Rite of Confession and Absolution was only the beginning of the service. We continued with an invocation of God's name and then began to pray. The prayers were prayers of protection and promise. They reminded those present of the protection they have in Jesus. As baptized children of God, Christians have been crucified with Christ and have risen with Him through the act of Holy Baptism.

There are many modern ideas about the promises God has attached to Baptism. These days, many Christians understand Baptism to be a work of man, an outward sign of the inward heart. To such Christians, Baptism is understood to be something the individual does rather than a work of God. Christians who come from this theological background will find it difficult to understand the great promise that other Christians find in Holy Baptism. The historic view of Baptism brings peace to the tormented soul. In this view, Baptism is the work of God. Baptism is understood to be the Word of God added to the physical element of water. Martin Luther, in his Small Catechism, teaches that the water without the promise of the Word is plain water. But with the Word of God, it is life-giving water, delivering the promise of life and salvation.

The main difference between these two distinct teachings comes down to the power and efficacy one ascribes to the Word of God. Does the Word alone have the power to create faith, or is it necessary to also have human activity? The deciding factor of this argument is best demonstrated by a church's teaching on the Baptism of infants. If a church teaches that an infant cannot and should not be baptized, then they root the efficacy of the Baptism within the one receiving it. In other words, Baptism becomes an outward sign of some inward quality. If a church accepts that the Word of God, attached to the water, is all that is necessary to create faith, then their faith is in the promise received. In this case, all of the activity is on God's part. Because God has connected Christians to Jesus' death and resurrection through Baptism, they can find great assurance, comfort, and hope in their Baptism.

To someone undergoing great spiritual doubt, such a gift is a great defense against the lies of Satan. Those lies had laid heavily upon Randy, but the words of forgiveness stood even stronger. Randy was a baptized child of God and the Invocation ("In the name of the Father and of the Son and of the Holy Spirit") stood as a confirmation of the words that were spoken over him on the day of his Baptism.

Following the prayers, the troubled man and his anxious sister joined together to sing "O Little Flock, Fear Not the Foe."[29] Just as the Confession and Absolution and the Invocation served an exorcistic function, so, too, did the hymn. Ridicule has long been known to cast Satan and his demons away. Stanza 3 declares, "Not earth nor hell's satanic crew Against us shall prevail. Their might? A joke, a mere facade! God is with us and we with God—Our vict'ry cannot fail." While Satan and his demonic crew continue to rail against the people of God, their defeat is already accomplished, and they know it. By singing this hymn, Randy was continuing to reinforce who he is in Jesus and what it means to be a baptized child of God. The power Satan was holding over this man for years was just a facade. The power of the devil seems too overpowering to withstand, but behind that powerful exterior Satan stands as one who has been judged and is no longer the prince of this world.

The exorcism liturgy continued with a series of four readings taken from Holy Scripture followed by a short sermon after each reading. The first three readings came from the Rite of Exorcism used in the Lutheran Church of Madagascar. The readings are included below with a short explanation:

THE FIRST READING—JOHN 14:12–17

> Truly, truly, I say to you, whoever believes in Me will also do the works that I do; and greater works than these will he do, because I am going to the Father. Whatever you ask in My name, this I will do, that the Father may be glorified in the Son. If you ask Me anything in My name, I will do it. If you love Me, you will keep My commandments. And I will ask the Father, and He will give you another Helper, to be with you forever, even the Spirit of truth, whom the world cannot receive, because it neither sees Him nor knows Him. You know Him, for He dwells with you and will be in you.

---

29 *LSB* 666. See the longer explanation of this hymn in chapter 1.

AFRAID

This text was chosen because it declares that God has promised to hear the prayers of His people when they speak in Jesus' name. It also promises the activity of the Holy Spirit when the Word of Jesus is proclaimed. Therefore, the person experiencing the exorcism hears the promise of Jesus and the demons hear of their doom in Jesus' name.

THE SECOND READING—MARK 16:15–20

And He said to them, "Go into all the world and proclaim the gospel to the whole creation. Whoever believes and is baptized will be saved, but whoever does not believe will be condemned. And these signs will accompany those who believe: in My name they will cast out demons; they will speak in new tongues; they will pick up serpents with their hands; and if they drink any deadly poison, it will not hurt them; they will lay their hands on the sick, and they will recover." So then the Lord Jesus, after He had spoken to them, was taken up into heaven and sat down at the right hand of God. And they went out and preached everywhere, while the Lord worked with them and confirmed the message by accompanying signs.

This second text continues to carry the theme of Baptism and the promise attached to it: "Whoever believes and is baptized will be saved." The significance of Baptism has already been discussed. Here once again, the troubled man received the promise of who he is in Baptism—that is, a child of God. The demons are also told that they have no right to this man, and they are then reminded that the exorcist is speaking the words "depart in the name of Jesus" not by his own authority but by the authority of Jesus.

THE THIRD READING—MATTHEW 18:18–20

Truly, I say to you, whatever you bind on earth shall be bound in heaven, and whatever you loose on earth shall be loosed in heaven. Again I say to you, if two of you agree on earth about anything they ask, it will be done for them by My Father in heaven. For where two or three are gathered in My name, there am I among them.

Matthew is direct and to the point. Jesus granted His pastors the authority to speak in His name. When they do so, their words carry the same authority as if Jesus is speaking them. Moreover, an exorcism should not be performed in isolation. At least one or more other Christians should be supporting the exorcist with their prayers. Hence, "Where two or three are gathered in My name, there am I among them." Once again, this is a reassurance for all people involved in the exorcism and a warning to the evil spirits present that Jesus is with the exorcist and his assistants.

THE FOURTH READING—JOHN 12:31–32

One additional reading was added that is not found in the Malagasy Exorcism Rite, but it proclaims the power of Jesus over Satan. The reading was taken from John 12:31–32, "Now is the judgment of this world; now will the ruler of this world be cast out. And I, when I am lifted up from the earth, will draw all people to Myself."

While it may appear that these verses have little to say about exorcism, this text represents the exorcism better than all others. As we stated earlier, the exorcism discussed in John's Gospel is a culmination of all the other exorcisms found within the New Testament Scriptures. It is the ultimate picture of the spiritual battle waged upon the earth. This text foreshadows the exorcism of Satan from his power upon the earth. Jesus is pointing to His own death upon the cross as an act of exorcism. At the cross, Jesus will dethrone Satan, casting him out. The accuser of men will lose his power because all sin is exonerated in Jesus' death. Satan has no say in the matter; if Jesus commands him to depart, he must surrender and leave the man in peace.

Following the readings and sermons, the service continued with the Lord's Prayer. Once again, this is an exorcistic prayer that culminates with the words, "Lead us not into temptation, but deliver us from evil." In his Large Catechism, Luther demonstrates that this petition might better be understood to read "deliver us from the evil one." Luther writes:

It looks like Jesus was speaking about the devil, like He would summarize every petition in one. So the entire substance of all our prayer is directed against our chief enemy. For it is he who hinders among us everything that we pray for: God's name or honor, God's kingdom and will, our daily bread, a cheerful good conscience, and so forth.[30]

Luther also understands the evil of this world. The world remains in the bondage of the devil and sin. Therefore, this petition is also acceptable in the more general form of "deliver us from evil." Luther writes:

But there is also included in this petition whatever evil may happen to us under the devil's kingdom: poverty, shame, death, and in short, all the agonizing misery and heartache of which there is such an unnumbered multitude on earth.[31]

As the words "deliver us from evil" concluded the prayer, the formal exorcism began:

Begone in the name of Jesus you evil spirits. You have no right to him, he is a child of God. He has received the name of the triune God upon his forehead and has been marked redeemed by God from sin, death, and you, you worthless devil. Be gone in the name of Jesus and trouble this man no more.

Following the Lord's Prayer and exorcism, I asked Randy to pray to Jesus for deliverance from sin, death, and the devil using his own words. Randy prayed, "Lord help me and drive all evil from me. You have called me by the Gospel through my Baptism and promised to be with me always. Lord Jesus Christ, cast this evil away by Your power and forgive me all my sins."

We concluded the service of exorcism with the exorcistic hymn "A Mighty Fortress Is Our God" (see ch. 1 for an explanation of the exorcistic

---

30 LC III 113.
31 LC III 115.

nature of the hymn). The hymn was written by Martin Luther and derives its content from Psalm 46: "Be still, and know that I am God. . . . The LORD of hosts is with us; the God of Jacob is our fortress" (vv. 10, 11). Luther writes:

> Though devils all the world should fill, All eager to devour us,
> We tremble not, we fear no ill, They shall not overpow'r us.
> This world's prince may still Scowl fierce as he will, He can
> harm us none. He's judged; the deed is done; One little word
> can fell him. (*LSB* 656:3)

Luther always thought it necessary to attack the pride of Satan, and his hymn does that masterfully. Where the name of Jesus is proclaimed, Satan doesn't stand a chance. Satan and his demons cannot stand in the presence of Jesus. Luther believes that Satan will take any opening we give him, but these words close those openings and lock the door. Satan has no power before the door that is Jesus (John 10:7).

So, what of the troubled man who underwent this exorcism? Was Randy possessed? No, he was not physically possessed, but he was severely oppressed by evil spirits. Was Randy also mentally ill? Probably. But such a diagnosis must be left to those who have the proper training and credentials. However, separating mental illness from the effects of sin and Satan implies a scientific and Rationalistic worldview that is not fitting with the biblical worldview. Randy may continue to suffer from mental illnesses in the future. Whatever the case, this man who entered the church filled with doubt about his salvation and forgiveness left the church that day with a great feeling of relief and peace. According to Randy, this was the first peace he had felt in many years. Even though Randy's sins were absolved, Satan is the great liar who will seek to bring despair back into Randy's life.

The only ongoing release and peace Randy can know will come with continued pastoral care. He will need continued catechesis in the Word of God, reception of the Sacraments,

---

Where the name of Jesus is proclaimed, Satan doesn't stand a chance.

---

participation in the fellowship of the Church, and a life of ongoing confession and absolution. These things were made clear to Randy, and he agreed to once again become active in his church.

One of the greatest dangers for the Christian is to avoid the Church. All Christians are involved in a spiritual battle; therefore, they are in need of Jesus' protection. This is especially true of those like Randy. Jesus warns:

> When the unclean spirit has gone out of a person, it passes through waterless places seeking rest, but finds none. Then it says, "I will return to my house from which I came." And when it comes, it finds the house empty, swept, and put in order. Then it goes and brings with it seven other spirits more evil than itself, and they enter and dwell there, and the last state of that person is worse than the first. (Matthew 12:43–45)

This warning stands before all Christians. Scripture states that all of us were once under the power of Satan before we received the gift of faith. Satan and his demons have been cast out of all of us either through Holy Baptism or the Word. Our only freedom from the devil and his demons is found in Jesus and the place where He has promised to be, the Church. To separate oneself from the Church is to separate oneself from the presence of the Lord of the Church, Jesus Christ, who died and rose again so as to destroy the works of the devil (1 John 3:8).

The Importance of Follow-Up

A few days after the exorcism, I called Randy to see how he was doing. Randy replied, "Things keep coming into my mind, and it is hard to keep them out, but I went for two walks outside by myself this week. I have not been outside walking by myself in years. It felt great." Randy even related how he was playing Christian hymns on his home organ. Janice added, "Pastor, he is doing better. He never talks on the phone, but he just talked to you."

Any improvement is just that, improvement. Previous talks with various pastors had no effect upon Randy. Medication and counseling had continually failed to help as well. He needed to confess his sins and hear the beautiful Words of Absolution. After only about forty minutes of pastoral care, Randy had begun to improve. Only time would tell if Randy would ever be able to overcome the torment of the years. But he had never shown any improvement at all until he underwent an exorcism. Even if Randy never totally recovers, being comforted, assured, and strengthened through the words of the Gospel, he can live without the despair that once laid so heavy upon him. He once again knows the comfort of his Baptism. He now has the ability to fight the spirits who return to speak doubt into his mind. Randy can now say, "Depart from me, devil, for Jesus has died upon a cross for the sin you attempt to torment me with. In His resurrection, Jesus has destroyed the power of death you threaten me with. Jesus has driven you from your throne of power. Leave me alone and trouble me no more."

Not what you expected? No, probably not what you expected at all. Why? Because, for most of us, the only thing we know about exorcism is what we have read in fictional accounts or watched on television, in the movies, and on the Internet. There was nothing sensational in Randy's exorcism. If anything, the only thing that may have seemed out of place from most Sunday worship services was the addition of the phrase, "Depart in the name of Jesus Christ." Nevertheless, everything done before that point was an exorcism in itself. Everything said, sung, and done pointed to the final proclamation: "Depart in the name of Jesus Christ." Jesus has defeated sin, death, and the devil. There is no reason for a Christian to fear or doubt the faithfulness of Jesus. He has promised to never leave us or forsake us. Jesus tells us where He is for us—that is, in the Divine Service, where His Word is spoken and His Sacraments are distributed. Do you want freedom from the sin of your flesh, the world, and the devil? You don't need to go looking for some type of mystical relief. Just come to the place where Jesus promises to be for you.

Chapter 9 Study Questions

1. What brought on the spiritual attacks that Randy described?

2. What is the evil eye? Should Christians worry about being cursed by others?

3. Why did Randy's home pastor avoid helping him when he learned of the spiritual attacks the man was enduring?

4. How did the Rite of Confession and Absolution provide comfort and release to Randy?

5. How is Confession and Absolution connected to exorcism?

6. Why did Randy find comfort in his Baptism?

7. What were the key elements of the short sermons preached during the exorcism?

8. What is it about the Lord's Prayer that is specifically exorcistic in nature?

9. How were Christian hymns used in the exorcism?

10. What do you think about the phrase "exorcism as liturgy"? Is this a new way of understanding the church service on Sunday morning?

11. What relief, if any, did Randy receive from the exorcism?

Sin is a curse that all of us are born into. Death is the result of that curse, and Jesus is the only rescue.

CHAPTER 10

An Ongoing Spiritual Battle

Submit yourselves therefore to God. Resist the devil, and he will flee from you. (James 4:7)

Many of the stories contained in this book have had positive outcomes. The people described in the stories attached themselves to various spiritualist movements and were later rescued from their despair by the Gospel. However, not all outcomes will end in such victorious ways. Christians have no doubt that even if they continue to face hardships of physical, emotional, or spiritual dimensions, they will always have the promise of Jesus. Jesus has placed His name upon them through Holy Baptism and sustained them through their journey in this life. He promises them that He has conquered sin, death, and the devil on their behalf. The forgiveness of sins and the promise of the resurrection await all who are in Jesus, no matter what they may face in this life. And yet, some may fall captive to the devil's lies and never receive a worldly peace.

I once had the opportunity to participate in a panel discussion on spiritual warfare. The panel consisted of various pastors, theologians, and missionaries. Each of the participants had extensive experience on the topic of exorcism. One pastor, who used to conduct exorcisms for his denomination, told the story of a woman whom he had been working with for more than a year. He told the group that she had been attached to the spiritualist movement and as a result had been possessed by multiple spirits. After spending a year with her, she seemed to be improving. The pastor knew that there was more work to do with her, but she had begun caring for her family and had returned to work. But what happened next was devastating to him and the rest of her family. One day as she was driving home from work, she deliberately drove her car off a bridge and committed suicide. She was dead, and there was nothing anyone could do to help her. As the pastor told the story, tears dripped from his eyes. "I could not help her," he told the group.

In the end, Jesus is the only exorcist, and pastors can only speak His words of freedom. Nevertheless, sin remains, and God, while not causing the pain of this world, allows terrible things to continue to occur. We live in a fallen world, and we are fallen people who are constantly seeking our own destruction. Sometimes we purposely hurt ourselves and others, and other times we do so unconsciously. Our Lord is our protector, but too often we seek to slip away from this protector and follow the desires of the flesh. Many times, we desire to retain evil in our lives knowing full well that it is evil.

Pastor, I Don't Want the Spirit to Leave Me

The next story is about a woman who has had a difficult life by anyone's standards. We will call this woman Doris. Doris grew up in an abusive home. Her family had deep ties with the spiritual movement through fortune-tellers. When she was a young girl, a close family member sexually molested her. Moreover, Doris had been raped multiple times during her teenage years. While mental illness did not run in her family, she had been diagnosed with depression at a young age. Such a diagnosis should not be surprising for a young woman who had experienced such horror in her life. Yet, mental illness and family problems were not the only problem with which this woman struggled.

"Pastor, the spirit is telling me to do horrible things," Doris told Pastor Jones at their first meeting. Doris had been seeing the spirit of a woman since she was a young girl and was now desperate for help. Pastor Jones asked Doris to tell him more about the spirit she claimed to be seeing and hearing. Doris told him that the spirit appeared to her when she was being raped as a young child. It spoke horrible things to her, things that are too horrible to describe in this book. Yet, at the same time, this spirit became her friend. It would come and speak with Doris, and sometimes it would turn on her and tell her to kill herself and others. Modern psychology would likely describe this woman as suffering from a dissociative condition. A psychologist might say that the spirit the woman saw was a way of coping with the trauma in her life. This may be true in some cases, but most within the mental health profession would fail to recognize demonic influences in the lives of people. It is difficult, if not impossible, to determine if a problem is only mental, only spiritual, or if it's both.

In most cases, there is a role for the mental health professional just as there is for the medical professional. Both of these vocations are instruments of God to do us good. Likewise, the pastor is to care for the soul of those entrusted into his care. Satan and his demons seek to destroy the entire person, body and soul. After much investigation, Pastor Jones decided that Doris was facing some severe spiritual problems in addition to her mental illness. Therefore, he would begin with a house blessing.

Pastor Jones arrived at her home in the early afternoon of the next day. Doris's family had been renting the home for the past few years. The home was unkempt. Strange religious pictures were hanging on the walls. Some of the pictures depicted crosses, others were of spirits. Above the doorway into Doris's bedroom was a piece of paper with the Lord's Prayer written in crayon. When asked about the paper, she said she placed it there in an attempt to keep the spirit from her bedroom, but it was unsuccessful. Such things happen frequently, as people attempt to use prayers as magic. Pastor Jones explained to Doris that prayer is more than words written on paper or spoken as a magical spell. Prayer is communication with God. In prayer, we speak to our divine Father as His own dear children, seeking help and giving thanks. Just like the words we use when bringing requests to our earthly fathers are important, so, too, are the words of our prayers to our heavenly Father. Jesus has given us the Lord's Prayer as a guideline for our prayers. The prayers we speak cannot deliver anything just by our speaking them. There is no power of intention as some might suggest.

Prayers of intention are becoming common in the nonbelieving world. The thought process goes like this: if enough people share a collective consciousness, those combined thoughts can produce a result. Such a use of prayer is idolatry. Our prayers or intentions have no power in themselves; God chooses to answer our prayers in accordance to His will, in whatever way He deems to be best in His own eyes. We simply trust in Him who has called us to be His children to be faithful and care for us as He has promised.

As Pastor Jones sat down at the kitchen table to talk, Doris continued to look over his shoulder. After a few minutes, he asked her if there was something wrong. Doris's response caught him a bit off guard. She said, "The spirit is standing behind you laughing and saying that you are lying. The spirit says that you cannot help me because I belong to her." After hearing these words, Pastor Jones began to pray in the name of Jesus. The words of the prayer went something like this:

> In the name of Jesus, leave this woman and her family alone, you evil spirit. She is a baptized child of God, and you have no authority over her. You are nothing other than a lying spirit, and there is no truth in you. Jesus has defeated you with His death upon the cross and His resurrection from the grave. You are weak and pitiful, without power over those who carry the name of Jesus upon their foreheads. Begone in Jesus' name. Amen.

There is nothing particularly special about this prayer over any other prayer. The point of the prayer was to disclose the lie of the evil spirit, point to the promises the baptized have in Jesus, and finally exorcize the spirit from the house in Jesus' name.

Following the prayer, Pastor Jones asked Doris if the evil spirit was still in the room. She replied, "As soon as you began to pray, the spirit left." (Just to be clear, Pastor Jones did not report seeing anything strange; everything appeared to be normal to him, but the woman claimed to see these things.) After some additional conversation, Pastor Jones began to go room to room speaking the words, "Begone in the name of Jesus." As he began the exorcism of the house, one of the children in the home, a young girl about seven years old, attempted to choke her pet guinea pig. She wrapped her hand around its tiny neck and laughed as she squeezed her hands. Her father rescued the animal from her hands. Seeing the young girl was disturbing, but Pastor Jones continued the blessing of the home. This was the first of three visits he made to the house. Each time he visited, the woman spoke about the spirit who would mock him until he began the prayers of exorcism.

On the last visit to the home, Doris admitted to him that she did not want the spirit to depart. She knew the spirit was evil, but it was her friend. Pastor Jones explained to her that he could not help her if she desired the spirits to remain. Yet, the bond she felt with the spirit was too strong for her to sever. That was the last time Doris asked her pastor to come to her home. A few months later, Pastor Jones was called to the local mental hospital to visit her. She had tried to commit suicide. Following a few weeks of treatment, she was released from the mental hospital under heavy medication and returned home.

Doris had not attended church since the last time Pastor Jones visited her home. Nevertheless, he tried to do what he could to keep in communication with her. After her release from the hospital, Doris began attending church regularly with her family. She sat in the pew every week, singing the hymns and receiving Holy Communion with her family by her side. This, too, was short lived, and after about a year, Doris's attendance once again began to slip. Before long, she and her family were attending church only once or twice per month. After a few more months, her husband stopped attending church altogether. When Pastor Jones inquired about his absence, Doris said that he had been placed in a mental hospital. When the pastor visited him, the husband described the spirits in the home and how they had asked him to do horrible things to his wife and children. He had finally experienced severe depression and attempted to commit suicide.

Eventually, things seemed to return to normal for the family. They said that everything was fine, but their assurances seemed odd. Pastor Jones suspected that things were not as normal as she had told him.

After a few months, Doris requested another pastoral visit. This time, she preferred to meet in the church office. Pastor Jones told her that she could come right over. When Doris entered the office, she looked much better than she had in the past. She had been visiting her psychiatrist and psychologist regularly. Her medications seemed to be helping her function much better. In past conversations, she always seemed distant, but now she was communicating quite well. Pastor Jones asked her what she wanted to talk about. Doris's answer caught him off guard: "Pastor, I want you to do an exorcism on me." He asked her why she wanted an exorcism, since she appeared to be doing well. But Doris responded, "My husband said if I don't get an exorcism he will leave me." Pastor Jones replied, "Why would he say that when you are doing so well?" She admitted that she did not understand why her husband was so insistent. She, too, thought she was doing better. Pastor Jones asked her if she had continued to see the spirit who had haunted her from her youth. Her response was what he had hoped for. Doris said, "No, I have not seen her in a long time." He asked her if she was having any suicidal thoughts. Doris once again said no. He asked her, "Why, then, would your husband want you to get an exorcism? You seem like you are doing far better than before." Doris agreed, "Yes, I do feel better, but my husband says I am worse than ever." Finally, Pastor Jones explained to her that she did not seem to have any signs of demonic possession or oppression, at least any that he could recognize. Yet, Doris was insistent, "Pastor, you must give me an exorcism; my husband will not let me come home until you do."

Doris obviously thought that she was possessed by a demon. Yet, pastors don't do exorcisms on demand. There needs to be a reason to believe that there is a demonic influence involved before an exorcism is performed. Sometimes people have great imaginations, and other times they suffer from psychiatric problems. In this case, it was clear that the woman had psychiatric problems, but the treatments seemed to be working well. She seemed to be doing fine. Pastor Jones was not about to do an exorcism on her just because her husband was demanding it. Pastor Jones tried to call her husband, but he refused to talk with him unless the pastor did as he had requested and exorcized the demons out of his wife. So the conversation ended in a stalemate. The husband still insisted that she needed an exorcism, but he agreed to allow her to return home.

Within a month, they returned to church without mention of exorcisms or spirits. While Pastor Jones suspected that there were still problems in the family, he concluded that the demonic problems had subsided. He wondered if Doris's problems were only mental and if he had misdiagnosed the initial spiritual problem. The medication seemed to be working, and she had not seen or heard from the spirit. At least, that was his thinking at the time.

A few months later, Pastor Jones received a strange phone call from one of the neighboring pastors. Doris had called him and requested an exorcism. He initially thought Doris belonged to his congregation, so he set up an appointment to visit her. This pastor serves a large church where it is difficult to know each of the members by name. After talking to Doris, he searched for her name in his church records and recognized that he had made a mistake. Doris did not belong to his church. Based on the address she had provided him, the neighboring pastor was calling to determine if Pastor Jones knew Doris. Pastor Jones told the neighboring pastor that she was the same woman that he had been dealing with for more than five years. The neighboring pastor explained that Doris said she knew Pastor

Jones and that he had denied her his help. After discussing Doris's case, the neighboring pastor agreed to call her back and cancel their appointment. He said that he would suggest that Doris call her own pastor to talk about how they should move forward. As Pastor Jones hung up the phone, his first thought was that Doris's husband must have been causing problems again. It was not as if he had not seen the woman recently. Doris had been attending church each week. He even remembered seeing Doris in church that past Sunday. He always made a point to stand in the narthex of the church and greet the families as they entered the church. That week, he had spoken to her, and she had told him everything was fine.

Within moments of hanging up, the office phone rang again. It was Doris. She asked for an appointment. Knowing it's best to handle problems as soon as possible, especially when there is a history of mental illness involved, he told her to come right over. As Pastor Jones waited for Doris to arrive, the phone in his office rang once again. This time, it was the neighboring pastor calling him back. He explained that the phone number he had for Doris would not work and asked if Pastor Jones could contact Doris on his behalf. Doris had contacted Pastor Jones without knowing that he had already talked to the neighboring pastor, or so it seemed anyway. Pastor Jones asked if he was sure that he had not talked to Doris following their earlier conversation. He said that he did not have Doris's phone number and had not spoken to her. The whole thing seemed a bit strange.

When Doris arrived in Pastor Jones's office, it was clear that something had changed since their last visit. Her eyes were dark and without a hint of emotion. In her hand were papers that appeared to be something she had printed from a website. They began the visit with prayer. Following the prayer, Pastor Jones asked Doris what, if anything, had recently changed in her life. She went on to tell him of an experience she recently had with a hypnotist. "I went to see the hypnotist because I knew there was something wrong with me." Pastor Jones asked her to explain to him what she meant. Doris then began to tell him about her issues with memory loss. "I cannot remember what I have done most days. When I come to church, I don't remember anything that was said in the sermon. The other day, my husband told me that I was talking to him in a strange voice and that I said, 'She is mine, and you will never get your wife back.'" She continued, "Pastor, I don't remember any of this. That is why I went to the hypnotist."

As she concluded her story, her appearance changed. Her face looked as if her life had been drained away from her, and she peered at her pastor without emotion. Feeling a bit uncomfortable, he tried to keep her talking. "How did things go at the hypnotist?" She replied, "I don't remember anything, but the hypnotist said my face changed, and I started to speak horrible things to her. She told my husband she could not help me and that he should go find a priest or pastor to help me." Pastor Jones asked her if that is why she called the neighboring pastor and asked for an appointment. She said that she did not remember calling the pastor. Rather than continuing to struggle with the issue of the phone call, Pastor Jones moved on to more important questions. He asked, "Have you seen the spirit we used to talk about anymore?" She told him that she had not seen the spirit in at least a year. "Well, that is good news," he said. She continued, "Pastor, I don't see her anymore, but now she is inside of me." He asked her if the spirit spoke to her anymore, and she said, "No, but my loved ones say she speaks through my voice. But I can't remember these things happening."

What was happening to this child of God? Was this simply a mental health issue? Pastor Jones asked Doris if she had spoken to her psychologist about this, and she stated that she had. What did her psychologist tell her to do? As it turns out, Doris's psychologist was a Christian and recognized that Doris was suffering from a spiritual problem. Therefore, the psychologist told Doris to go see her pastor.

The way Doris was looking at Pastor Jones changed. She looked like she had an underlying evil grin appearing and disappearing from her face. Before long, Pastor Jones was questioning whether he was imagining this or not. Trying to change the subject, he asked Doris about the papers she continued to clutch between her fingers. Without a word, she handed them to him. Some were printouts from various charismatic websites that described various types of spirits that could possess people. Other pages spoke of the relationship between generational curses and spirit possession. As her pastor looked at the papers, Doris spoke up, "Pastor, I have a generational curse!"

The topic of generational curses was discussed earlier in this book. We last encountered the term when we heard the story of Jill, the woman who had welcomed the voodoo priest into her home. The concept of a generational curse comes from the occult. It is usually diagnosed through a medium or declared by a possessing spirit. Both of these sources should be ignored. Satan is the father of lies (John 8:44). It is hard to believe that Christians who have been warned by God through the Holy Scriptures would ignore the truth of God and believe a lying spirit.

Some charismatic Christians and Roman Catholics claim that because they have "bound the spirit" with the Word of God, it can no longer lie to them. To be clear, there is no biblical precedence for such things. Yet, in spite of the danger, they go on to interrogate the spirit or spirits about the spirit world. They ask questions regarding the hidden workings of life, death, ghosts, curses, and other occult topics. Such conversations are harmful to the Christian faith. As a result of such conversations, Christians have begun to heed the words of demons over the clear revealed Word of God. This woman had fallen into this false theology. Doris believed that she had a generational curse and, because of the curse, that there was no hope for her.

In one sense, we are all under the generational curse placed upon Adam and Eve. Sin is a curse that all of us are born into. Death is the result of that curse, and Jesus is the only rescue. So how should one view the topic of generational curses? The last place a Christian should look for an answer is in the mouth of a deceiving spirit. The only reliable answer is found in Jesus and His revealed Word. So how should one respond if someone claims to be under a generational curse? The questions used by Doris's pastor are a good starting point:

1. Are you baptized? If so, what does this mean about your relationship to God? (See Roman 6:3–4.)

2. Do you trust in Jesus? What does His crucifixion do to the power of the devil? (See John 12:31.)

3. Who is more powerful: Jesus? or Satan and his demons? (See Colossians 1:15–18.)

4. In light of these passages and others, can Christians have a generational curse that places them into the control of Satan as his property?

After spending some time reviewing these questions with her pastor, Doris began to understand who she was in Jesus. She was baptized. The name of the triune God was added to the water, and she was made a child of God. If she belonged to God, could she belong to the devil or his demons? She agreed that she could not. Does she trust in Jesus? Does she come to church? Does she receive Holy Communion? Does she pray? Doris confessed her faith in Jesus, His death, and resurrection. Yes, she attended church. Yes, Doris looked forward to receiving Holy Communion. Yes, Doris was constantly praying.

The purpose of these questions was not to focus the woman on her personal piety but only to show her that God had brought her to faith through His Gospel and that she was living her life as a Christian. If she is connected to Jesus' death and resurrection through her Baptism (Romans 6:3–4) and if Jesus had defeated the devil in His crucifixion and resurrection (John 12:31), how could the devil claim any ownership over her?

After considering these questions and their relevancy to her situation, Doris recognized that the only way she could be under the power of a generational curse was if she or someone else had given her into the devil's hands. With this revelation, Pastor Jones then asked her, "Who would have such power?" If she is the property of Jesus, only Jesus could give her up, but He did the exact opposite. Rather than giving her up, He rescued her from sin, death, and the devil. Of all of the questions listed, question 3 is meant to eliminate any doubt as to the power of Jesus over the devil and his demons. *Who is more powerful: Jesus? or Satan and his demons?*

The Letter to the Colossians is clear about the power Jesus has over the devil, his demons, and all of creation:

> He is the image of the invisible God, the firstborn of all creation. For by Him all things were created, in heaven and on earth, visible and invisible, whether thrones or dominions or rulers or authorities—all things were created through Him and for Him. And He is before all things, and in Him all things hold together. And He is the head of the body, the church. He is the beginning, the firstborn from the dead, that in everything He might be preeminent. For in Him all the fullness of God was pleased to dwell, and through Him to reconcile to Himself all things, whether on earth or in heaven, making peace by the blood of His cross. And you, who once were alienated and hostile in mind, doing evil deeds, he has now reconciled in His body of flesh by His death, in order to present you holy and blameless and above reproach before Him, if indeed you continue in the faith, stable and steadfast, not shifting from the hope of the gospel that you heard, which has been proclaimed in all creation under heaven, and of which I, Paul, became a minister. (Colossians 1:15–23)

Doris agreed Jesus is the Lord of all things. Now that she understood who she was in Jesus, she recognized that Scripture does not allow for a belief in generational curses. Nevertheless, Satan remains the father of lies. Therefore, the devil is crafty and persistent as he tries to persuade Christians to believe his lies.

Doris had entered into the bondage of the devil's lies, but it was not necessary for her to remain a captive. Pastor Jones explained to her that when a Christian believes she has a generational curse, she is accepting this lie. Using a series of examples, he demonstrated his point. He asked, "If a man were to come to your house and take away your car, would you let him do it?" The answer is, of course, no! Why? Because he doesn't have that authority. Although, if he showed up at your house with a court order, and he told you he was an officer of the court, your response might be different. More than likely, you would hand your car over to him. If you doubted his credentials, you might call the police to check on his story. If he fooled you, he would have possession of your car, but that does not mean he would have a right to it. The same holds true for the lies of Satan. He is very crafty and capable of convincing people of his lies, but in the end they are still only lies. The truth is that all who are baptized children of God belong to God. There is no way of separating them from God (Romans 8). If one belongs to Jesus, Satan cannot claim ownership. Nevertheless, if Satan and his demons trick someone into believing that they are under the control of devil, that person will follow their false slave master even though their slavery is a lie.

Doris continues to struggle with the lies of Satan, her mental illness, and the problems of her past and will continue to require pastoral care for some time into the future. While it is impossible to be certain if Doris will ever become free from these torments, she is a child of God, and therefore her salvation is not in question. At the end, she will enter into eternal life and receive the promise of the glory that awaits all of God's saints in heaven. This story is a reminder that spiritual warfare is part of many Christians' lives. Some will have clear victories, others will undergo a lifelong series of difficult battles, and still others will endure worldly defeat. Yet, for the Christian, the final battle is won in Jesus Christ.

Chapter 10 Study Questions

1. Why is it necessary to remember that Jesus is the only exorcist?

2. Can spiritual problems and mental problems always be differentiated? Explain your answer.

3. Doris had a deep affection for the Lord's Prayer. What was the problem identified in this chapter with her use of this most holy prayer?

4. Review the exorcistic prayer provided in this chapter. What key points can you identify in this prayer?

5. Should pastors perform exorcisms on anyone who asks for them?

6. Should a Christian avoid hypnotism? Why or why not? Explain your answer.

7. Can the words of a demon be trusted? What about those demons that are "bound" by the Word of God to speak the truth by the exorcist?

8. Is it possible for a Christian to be under the power of a generational curse?

9. What four questions does this chapter offer to help those who worry about being under a generational curse?

10. What does Colossians 1:15–23 teach us about the authority of Jesus over the devil and his demons?

We have no authority over the devil, but we stand in the stead of the One who has ultimate authority over all of creation—namely, Jesus.

CHAPTER 11

AN IMPROPER RESPONSE

So hearken now, thou miserable devil, adjured by the name
of the eternal God and of our Savior Jesus Christ, and depart
trembling and groaning, conquered together with thy hatred,
so that thou shalt have nothing to do with the servant of God.
(Martin Luther, AE 53:98)

One of the most difficult issues related to the topic of spiritual warfare is the uncertainty that always follows. We usually don't have the answers we desire. Is the problem being faced simply a problem of one's fallen state? Is the problem physical, mental, imaginary? Is the problem demonic? Is the answer to the problem a combination of all of the above? Except in the case of rare and dramatic circumstances, it is usually impossible to answer these questions. For those who come from a Western background, the lack of knowing is frustrating.

Generally, it is easier to deal with the problems described in this book from a medical or scientific perspective. If we can place these problems into a scientific category, there is a high possibility that we can find an answer. For instance, when faced with a medical problem, doctors can run various test until they identify the problem or at least find a medication that treats the person's condition. The Christian cannot exclude the possibility of a spiritual cause especially when the problem presents itself as a spiritual problem.

If one does not believe in demons, the prospect of exorcism seems at best fanciful and at worst harmful. Still, to look for demonic problems in every circumstance is equally troubling. Sin has brought death to this world and the symptoms of death are found in the sickness and phobias that plague humanity. Demon possession remains, for now, a rare occurrence. Most of the people pastors serve in their ministry are suffering under the curse of sin, which is common to all. Therefore, it is important to seek medical attention whenever someone reports experiencing what the scientific world would call visual or auditory hallucinations. Yet for too long, the Church in the West has simply referred its members to the medical field and washed its hands of the problem. Some within the Church take a different route. For example, Pentecostalism and those holding to a charismatic spiritual orientation too often claim demons are at the center of many problems ranging from lust, theft, murder, pornography, alcoholism, and drug addiction. Other Christians have become Christian animists seeking out magical spells and protections that have a connection to the occult. The following stories represent what I would call an inappropriate response.

Why Is There Salt under the Bed?

This story took place in a small rural congregation with a limited budget. The congregation was going through the process of finding a new pastor after their pastor of many years had retired. They asked their district for assistance by providing an interim pastor to serve them until a new pastor could be found. Being a congregation with limited budget, they no longer owned a parsonage. The district informed them that while a pastor was available to serve them during the calling process, they would need to provide a place for the pastor to live. Fortunately, a local congregation had a parsonage that was vacant, so they contracted with the church to rent the parsonage for one year.

Soon after moving into the rented parsonage, the interim pastor began experiencing what he called demonic problems in the house. The problems were mainly focused in the master bedroom where he and his wife slept. Both reported being awakened from their sleep to see a dark shadowy figure.

The pastor had retired from full-time service as a chaplain at a large mental hospital. As a result of his work at the hospital, he had experienced many instances of spiritual warfare and demon possession. He, like most pastors, had not been formally trained in how to deal with the problem of demon possession. What he knew came from books on the occult and the counsel of Roman Catholic priests he had encountered over his many years in the Holy Ministry. The pastor never mentioned these problems to the congregation; instead, he dealt with them as he thought best.

After a few months, the congregation found a new permanent pastor. Because of their financial difficulties, they were only able to offer a small salary with few benefits. But they decided to continue the rental agreement with the neighboring congregation, which they then provided as a portion of their new pastor's compensation package.

The new pastor's wife was pregnant with her fourth child when he and his family moved into the house, and at first everything was going well. But after the birth of their new baby, the pastor's wife began experiencing postpartum depression. It was not long before her worsening symptoms led them to seek out clinical care. Her doctor prescribed short-term residential treatment and antidepressants. But her experience was more than just postpartum depression. . . .

Since the congregation had already furnished the rental house for the interim pastor and the new pastor's bed would not fit up the narrow stairway of the older house, he did not immediately move in his family's own furniture. However, after the birth of the new baby the pastor decided to make his wife more comfortable by moving their own bed into the master bedroom. When the time came to remove the old bed, a large amount of salt poured out from around the perimeter of the box spring under the mattress.

Finding the salt strange and expecting that there was some sort of spiritual meaning behind the practice, the new pastor contacted the former interim pastor to inquire the meaning of the salt. The interim pastor claimed that he had spoken exorcistic words over the salt before he poured it between the mattress and the box spring to keep evil spirits away from him and his wife as they slept.

I have met many well-meaning pastors who have become "Christian animists" without ever realizing what they were doing. Animism is about power. The word comes from the Latin word *anima*, which means "breathe" or "soul." A Christian animist is one who ascribes power to words or items that God has not commanded.

Like many people in our culture, that pastor who poured salt between his mattress and box spring was afraid. Salt cannot keep the evil spirits away; even experienced pastors get these things wrong sometimes. That is why this story is listed under the title, "An Improper Response." He was never taught how to deal with the problem of the demonic. He began following the Roman Ritual (the exorcism ritual of the Roman Catholic Church) and employing methods from popular demonologists. Luther and the reformers warned pastors about following such measures. The early baptismal rite of 1523 that Luther used contained a section where

---

A Christian animist is one who ascribes power to words or items that God has not commanded.

---

salt was used, but its use was purely symbolic. However, Luther removed that section of the baptismal liturgy when he reedited the baptismal liturgy in 1526.

For those curious about the prayer attached to the 1523 baptismal rite that used the salt, it begins with the officiate blowing three times under the child's eyes and saying, "Depart thou unclean spirit and give room to the Holy Spirit."[32] Following the first of the exorcisms, the sign of the cross is then marked upon the forehead and upon the heart of the baptized. Satan is then cast out of the person as he is marked as one of God's children. The following prayer is a commentary of the exorcism administered during the Baptism:

> O Almighty eternal God, Father of our Lord Jesus Christ, look upon N., thy servant whom thou hast called to instruction in the faith, drive away from him all blindness of his heart, break all the snares of the devil with which he is bound, open to him, Lord, the door of thy grace: So that marked with the sign of thy wisdom he may be freed of the stench of all evil lusts and serve thee joyfully according to the sweet savor of thy commandments in thy church and grow daily and be made meet to come to the grace of thy baptism to receive the balm of life; through Christ our Lord. Amen.[33]

Salt is offered as the prayers continue:

> Therefore, thou miserable devil, acknowledge thy judgment and give glory to the true and living God, give glory to His Son Jesus Christ and to the Holy Ghost, and depart from this N., his servant; for God and our Lord Jesus Christ has of his goodness called him to his holy grace and blessing, and to the fountain of baptism so that thou mayest never dare to disturb this sign of the holy cross + which we make on his forehead; through Him who cometh again to judge, etc.

32 AE 53:96.
33 AE 53:96.

So hearken now, thou miserable devil, adjured by the name of the eternal God and of our Savior Jesus Christ, and depart trembling and groaning, conquered together with thy hatred, so that thou shalt have nothing to do with the servant of God who now seeks that which is heavenly and renounces thee and thy world, and shall live in blessed immortality. Give glory therefore now to the Holy Ghost who cometh and descendeth from the loftiest castle of heaven in order to destroy thy deceit and treachery, and having cleansed the heart with the divine fountain, to make it ready, a holy temple and dwelling of God, so that this servant of God, freed from all guilt of former sin, may always give thanks to the eternal God and praise his name forever and ever. Amen.[34]

While Luther did not find such an action to be heretical, he understood the potential for error that could result in blessing objects other than divinely mandated elements in the Sacraments of Baptism and the Lord's Supper.[35]

The interim pastor had not been thinking about ancient baptismal rites when he put a perimeter of salt around his bed. He was simply trying to protect his wife and himself from the demonic spirit that harassed them. Yet, without knowing it, he was falling into one of Satan's oldest and greatest tricks. Satan is always ready to direct God's children away from the Word and promise of God so that they instead look to idols. Luther warns, "Satan is so successful in disguising himself into an angel of light (2 Cor. 11:14) and into the image of God that he entices us away from prayer and the Word and then attacks and overpowers us in our nude and helpless condition."[36]

---

34 AE 53:97–98.

35 Bryan D. Spinks, *Reformation and Modern Rituals and Theologies of Baptism: From Luther to Contemporary Practices* (Aldershot, England: Ashgate, 2006), 11.

36 AE 13:109–10.

With the best of intentions, the interim pastor had unknowingly made the salt into an idol. Similarly, the same thing can be said about holy water, incense, and other religious symbols when improperly used. In chapter 2, I shared the story of the voodoo priest who used salt and water in his magical rite. It might be helpful to return to that section and reread the nature of the voodoo priest's rite. Even the people of God fall for such lies. Luther is helpful in this area as he writes, "In relation to God idols are no joke. Such idols in the heart are false righteousness, glory in works, unbelief, and anything else that takes the place of Christ in the heart in the form of unbelief."[37] Luther specifically warns pastors against using the Roman Rite of Exorcism. Luther did not deny demonic possession or have a problem using the power of Jesus' name in connection with exorcism; his problem with the Roman Ritual was the idolatry and superstitions that accompanied it.[38] Superstition always leads to idolatry, even for well-meaning pastors and members of the Christian Church.

While the point of this story is to demonstrate the inappropriate actions that well-meaning people can fall into, some of the readers are no doubt wondering about the pastor and his wife who found the salt around the mattress in their new home. The new pastor and his wife never experienced any strange behavior in the house in terms of seeing or hearing any strange things. However, after learning the background of the house and the interim pastor's experiences, the new pastor exorcized the house using one of the traditional house-blessing rites found in his *Lutheran Service Book: Agenda*.[39]

When the pastor's wife began to overcome the depression, she remembered the point when she gave into the depression and how it "grabbed

---

37 AE 40:94–95.

38 The introduction to the English translation of the Roman Ritual agrees with Luther that the medieval rite was loaded with "practices that were superstitious to an extreme." The introduction goes on to admit that many medieval magical practices have been introduced into the Roman Ritual. See Philip T. Weller, trans., *The Roman Ritual*, Complete Edition (Milwaukee: Bruce Publishing, 1964), 638.

39 See *Lutheran Service Book: Agenda* (St. Louis: Concordia, 2006).

hold of her." Did she experience a spiritual attack under the cover of depression? Sometimes there is no way of knowing. While a house blessing, or exorcism, is never inappropriate, those dealing with issues of depression should always seek out those who have the vocations that God has provided to deal with such issues—namely, a medical doctor or mental health professional.

Should We Ridicule the Devil or Not?

Anyone who has read the works of Dr. Martin Luther has likely noticed that he constantly speaks about attacking the pride of Satan, or, in other words, ridiculing the devil. Many pastors find the behavior of ridiculing the devil and his demons to be inconsistent with Holy Scripture. They struggle with Luther's constant urging to do so because of the example in Jude 1:9, in which the archangel Michael deals with the devil. The text states:

> But when the archangel Michael, contending with the devil, was disputing about the body of Moses, he did not presume to pronounce a blasphemous judgment, but said, "The Lord rebuke you."

There is actually no contradiction, just a different emphasis. It is most certainly important to hold to the authority of Holy Scripture over the writings of Martin Luther. Anyone who is a Christian should concede this point. Yet, it is not necessary to discount Martin Luther's understanding of ridicule with Jude's account of the events surrounding the body of Moses. The answer to the seeming contradiction lies in understanding that Luther is not ridiculing the devil by offering a personal assault, as one person ridicules another. Luther ridicules the devil by speaking of his defeat by Jesus on the cross.

The text from Jude refers to the interaction between the archangel Michael and the devil. It speaks about the angel's intentional refusal to rebuke the devil. Instead of personally rebuking the devil, he says, "The Lord rebuke you." Does such a text nullify Luther's encouragement to ridicule the devil? Before we answer this question, we must determine the historical timeline of this event. Does the interaction between Michael and the devil take place before or after the crucifixion and resurrection of Jesus? If it takes place before the crucifixion event, it would make sense for Michael to leave the rebuking of the devil up to the Lord. Scripture represents the devil as the prince of this world (Ephesians 2:2) and the ruler of the world before the crucifixion (John 12:31), therefore granting the devil a "status." Jesus is clear that through the crucifixion, the devil loses his status:

> "Now is the judgment of this world; now will the ruler of this world be cast out. And I, when I am lifted up from the earth, will draw all people to Myself." He said this to show by what kind of death He was going to die. (John 12:31–33)

Following Jesus' death, resurrection, and ascension, the Church was sent out into the world with the purpose of making disciples, baptizing, and teaching (Matthew 28:19–20; Mark 16:15; Luke 24:47). Moreover, the apostles, and later the pastors of the Church, are sent out to speak on behalf of Jesus:

> Jesus said to them again, "Peace be with you. As the Father has sent Me, even so I am sending you." And when He had said this, He breathed on them and said to them, "Receive the Holy Spirit. If you forgive the sins of any, they are forgiven them; if you withhold forgiveness from any, it is withheld." (John 20:21–23)

Jesus' crucifixion and resurrection made it so that through preaching, teaching, absolving, and administering the Sacraments, the Church is constantly ridiculing Satan. These gifts not only bring eternal benefits to those who hear and receive them but also continue to mock the devil as one who has been cast out of his position of power. If we understand Luther's advice to ridicule the devil as one speaking in the stead of the Lord, his advice is well taken (Jude 1:9).

> We have no authority over the devil, but we stand in the stead of the One who has ultimate authority over all of creation—namely, Jesus.

There are many problems associated with sinful human beings attempting to rebuke the devil using magical rites and animistic rituals. Those making such rebukes risk great harm. Those who contend with the devil in his realm (Ephesians 2:2) are sure to lose. In his book *Grace Upon Grace: Spirituality for Today*, John Kleinig provides helpful advice to those who seek to interact with the devil and his demons. He writes,

> Those who confess Christ do not need to go on a crusade against Satan and seek out his strongholds in their social environment. He seeks them out and relentlessly hunts them down.[40]

The ridicule of Satan should only take place in times of spiritual attack, never in jest or out of sinful pride but only in view of the victory of Christ Jesus through the crucifixion and resurrection. Dr. Kleinig's words are helpful here as well, "Subordination to the authority of Christ is the foundation for success in spiritual warfare, for at its core it has to do with authority rather than knowledge and power."[41]

We have no authority over the devil, but we stand in the stead of the One who has ultimate authority over all of creation—namely, Jesus. The Church recognizes this authority in the absolution of sins. The pastor stands and speaks as a messenger of Jesus. The announcement of forgiveness is spoken by the lips of the pastor, but they deliver the saving words of Jesus. Likewise, the same authority of Jesus is behind the rebukes of the devil when spoken by the pastor.

---

40 John W. Kleinig, *Grace Upon Grace: Spirituality for Today* (St. Louis: Concordia, 2008), 232.
41 Kleinig, *Grace Upon Grace*, 250.

Chapter 11 Study Questions

1. Why do people find it more desirable to seek answers from science rather than faith when dealing with the possibility of visual or audio hallucinations?

2. What did the interim pastor do wrong according to this chapter?

3. What possible problems did Martin Luther find with the blessing of objects?

4. How are religious practices involving the use of holy water and other religious symbols problematic when used within the context of exorcism?

5. Should an exorcism ever take the place of medical attention? Explain your answer.

6. Should one use ridicule against the devil and his demons when engaged in a spiritual battle?

7. What does the chapter suggest to be the only foundation for success when one is involved in spiritual warfare?

If Christians do not recognize the fallen nature of the world, they will not only fall into its traps but will also seek answers in the wrong places.

CONCLUSION

ANSWERS FOR A SOCIETY IN FEAR

I tell you, My friends, do not fear those who kill the body, and after that have nothing more that they can do. But I will warn you whom to fear: fear Him who, after He has killed, has authority to cast into hell. (Luke 12:4–5)

What has been presented here is an introduction into the problem of demon possession and spiritual warfare in American Christianity, specifically focusing on the lives of those who have fallen prey to the attacks of the devil and his demons. Some, after reading this book, will continue to doubt the reality of the spiritual war that faces humanity. Nevertheless, many Christians have been searching for the answers provided within these pages. Those answers are sure to stimulate new questions. Some Christians will struggle with the emphasis placed on the performative nature of the preached Word of Jesus, along with the heavy emphasis placed on Confession and Absolution and the Sacraments of Holy Baptism and the Lord's Supper. The doctrine of Jesus' presence, which confesses that Jesus attached Himself to His Word and to His Sacraments, is foreign to many evangelical Christians. Nevertheless, Jesus' presence is the only hope or power that can free someone from spiritual bondage. As such, the case studies in this book are meant to demonstrate how the Word of God attached to the Sacraments, the divine liturgy, and pastoral care brings comfort and peace to the lives of God's people.

Another point of this book was to encourage people to look at the world around them through a more spiritual lens, recognizing the spiritual dangers in which they, and others, find themselves. The world in which we live is not spiritually neutral. There is evil in this world, and behind that evil is the devil and all his demons. It is true that humanity is included in this evil, but Satan and his demons stand behind that evil. St. Paul makes this clear in Ephesians 6:12 when he speaks of the central problem of this world; namely, the cosmic powers over this present darkness, and the spiritual forces of evil in the heavenly places. If Christians do not recognize the fallen nature of the world, they will not only fall into its traps but will also seek answers in the wrong places. Any spiritual answer that does not have at its center the work of Jesus upon the cross and the empty tomb of the resurrection is a lie—and behind that lie is the devil.

One additional point the reader should take away from this book is the problem with Christian animism. When someone ascribes power to words or items that God has not commanded, he or she falls for the lie of Satan, who seeks to nullify the Sacraments that Christ Jesus has instituted and raise in their place false sacraments of his devising. One of the most common and dangerous forms of Christian animism is prayer. Prayer becomes a problem when we begin to ascribe power to the words prayed rather than to the One who promises to hear the prayers. The only power prayer has for the Christian is the power of the promise that God has made

---

If Christians do not recognize the fallen nature of the world, they will not only fall into its traps but will also seek answers in the wrong places.

AFRAID

to hear the prayers of His saints and answer them as a dear Father. Such a promise is a great blessing and brings comfort to every Christian. When prayer is elevated to a Means of Grace, the place of the preached Word and Sacraments, it has transitioned into something for which it was not intended. The point here is that God has promised to act on our behalf through His Word and Sacraments and not through prayer, words spoken by the Christian. The difference between prayer and the Word and Sacraments—the Means of Grace—is that the Means of Grace have real power to deliver life and forgiveness. Through these gifts, faith is created and the devil is cast away.

Everything presented in this book is based upon the doctrine that God has declared the Christian righteous because of the work of Jesus. As a result of this righteousness, Christians have a new standing before God. Rather than standing in the sin that continues to cling to them, they stand in the holiness of Jesus, who has covered them with His righteousness. This is the doctrine of justification. For Christians who recognize this truth, the gates of hell have been driven away, and life carries a new meaning. Without the fear that death brings only annihilation or eternal punishment, Christians begin to recognize that while they will still find themselves in times of weakness and fear, Jesus is there by their side and will not leave them alone. Even as sin, death, and the devil appear to be winning the battle, the cross of Jesus and the empty tomb declare their victory. We have nothing to fear from this world or the devil. Such is Jesus' promise on Easter morning. Fear has no place when sins are forgiven and death is destroyed.

The greatest weapon the Christian has against the fears of this world and the spiritual attacks of the devil is his Baptism. In the waters of Baptism, the Christian dies with Jesus, is raised to new life, and is promised that he will rise to be with Jesus in eternity. Therefore, "Do not be afraid" (Matthew 28:10), and "Peace be with you" (John 20:19; cf. Luke 24:36–39). These are the first words that Jesus spoke at His resurrection, and they continue to resound in the ears of the baptized, calming our fear and giving us hope today.

Appendix: Exorcistic Hymns

The following chart lists hymns found in *Lutheran Service Book* that are exorcistic in nature.

Hymn Number	Hymn Title
349	Hark the Glad Sound
357	O Come, O Come, Emmanuel
372	O Jesus Christ, Thy Manger Is (see st. 3)
375	Come, Your Hearts and Voices Raising
378	Break Forth, O Beauteous Heavenly Light (see st. 1)
383	A Great and Mighty Wonder (see st. 5)
394	Songs of Thankfulness and Praise (see st. 3)
418	O Lord, throughout These Forty Days
419	Savior, When in Dust to Thee
421	Jesus, Grant That Balm and Healing
436	Go to Dark Gethsemane
447	Jesus, in Your Dying Woes
448	O Darkest Woe (see st. 6)
458	Christ Jesus Lay in Death's Strong Bands
464	The Strife Is O'er, the Battle Done (see st. 2)
467	Awake, My Heart, with Gladness
480	He's Risen, He's Risen (see st. 3)
488	He Is Arisen! Glorious Word
494	See, the Lord Ascends in Triumph (see st. 2)
502	Holy Spirit, the Dove Sent from Heaven
505	Triune God, Be Thou Our Stay
508	The Day Is Surely Drawing Near
513	The Clouds of Judgment Gather (see st. 1)
514	The Bridegroom Soon Will Call Us (see st. 3)
521	Christ, the Lord of Hosts, Unshaken
533	Jesus Has Come and Brings Pleasure (see st. 3)
541	"Away From Us!" the Demon Cried

544	O Love, How Deep (see st. 3)
556	Dear Christians, One and All, Rejoice (see st. 2)
557	Seek Where You May to Find a Way (see st. 1)
561	The Tree of Life
574	Before the Throne of God Above (see st. 3)
577	Almighty God, Your Word Is Cast (see st. 2)
580	The Gospel Shows the Father's Grace (see st. 4)
585	Lord Jesus Christ, with Us Abide (see st. 4)
587	I Know My Faith Is Founded (see st. 2)
594	God's Own Child, I Gladly Say It
599	O Gracious Lord, with Love Draw Near (see st. 3)
627	Jesus Christ, Our Blessed Savior
656 and 657	A Mighty Fortress Is Our God
663	Rise, My Soul, to Watch and Pray
665	Be Strong in the Lord
666	O Little Flock, Fear Not the Foe
668	Rise! To Arms! With Prayer Employ You
690	Hope of the World
703	How Can I Thank You, Lord (see st. 2)
708	Lord, Thee I Love with All My Heart
714	Who Trusts in God a Strong Abode
716	I Walk in Danger All the Way
718	Jesus, Lead Thou On
721	Lead Me, Guide Me (see st. 2)
724	If God Himself Be for Me
743	Jesus, Priceless Treasure
752	Be Still, My Soul
758	The Will of God Is Always Best (see st. 3)
763	When Peace, like a River (see st. 2)
766	Our Father, Who from Heaven Above (see st. 3)
850	God of Grace and God of Glory
860	Gracious Savior, Grant Your Blessing (see st. 1)

869	With the Lord Begin Your Task (see st. 2)
874	O Splendor of God's Glory Bright (see st. 3)
876	O Blessed, Holy Trinity (see st. 2)
877	God, Who Made the Earth and Heaven
878	Abide with Me (see st. 5)
880	Now Rest beneath Night's Shadow (see st. 4)
882	O Christ, Who Art the Light and Day
884	Lord, Support Us All Day Long (see st. 2)
903	This Is the Day the Lord Has Made (see st. 2)
919	Abide, O Dearest Jesus
947	All Glory Be to God on High
957	Our Father Who Art in Heaven — I
958	Our Father Who Art in Heaven — IIa

Bibliography

Baptist Distinctives. "Is Soul Competency *The* Baptist Distinctive?" baptistdistinctives.org/articles/is-soul-competency-the-baptist-distinctive/ (accessed May 19, 2014).

Bennett, Robert H. *I Am Not Afraid: Demon Possession and Spiritual Warfare: True Accounts from the Lutheran Church of Madagascar.* St. Louis: Concordia, 2013.

Berry, Thomas. "Classical Western Spirituality and the American Experience." *Cross Currents* (Winter 1981).

Bloom, Harold. *The American Religion: The Emergence of the Post-Christian Nation.* New York: Simon and Schuster, 1992.

Coeckelbergh, Mark. "The Spirit in the Network: Models for Spirituality in a Technical Culture." *Zygon: Journal of Religion and Science* 45, no. 4 (2010): 957–78.

Das, A. Andrew. *Baptized into God's Family: The Doctrine of Infant Baptism for Today.* Milwaukee: Northwestern, 1991.

Fisk, Jonathan M. *Broken: 7 Christian Rules That Every Christian Ought to Break as Often as Possible.* St. Louis: Concordia, 2012.

Frederickson, Bruce G. *Satanism.* How to Respond to World Religions. St. Louis: Concordia, 1995.

Haraldsson, Erlendur, and Joop M. Houtkooper. "Traditional Christian Beliefs, Spiritualism, and the Paranormal: An Icelandic-American Comparison." *The International Journal for the Psychology of Religion* 6, no. 1 (1996): 51–64.

Hemingway, Mollie Ziegler. "Faith Unbounded: Why Spirituality Is Sexy but Religion Is Not." *Christianity Today*, September 20, 2010.

Horowitz, Mitch. *Occult America: The Secret History of How Mysticism Shaped Our Nation.* New York: Bantam Books, 2009.

Humphrey, Edith M. "It's Not About Us: Modern Spirituality Begins and Ends with the Self." *Christianity Today*, April 2, 2001.

Kleinig, John W. *Grace Upon Grace: Spirituality for Today.* St. Louis: Concordia, 2008.

Kolb, Robert. *Luther and the Stories of God: Biblical Narratives as a Foundation for Christian Living.* Grand Rapids, MI: Baker Academic, 2012.

Krause, Neal. "Reported Contact with the Dead, Religious Involvement, and Death Anxiety in Late Life." *Review of Religious Research* 52, no. 4 (June 1, 2011): 347–64.

Kraus, Rachel. "The Many Faces of Spirituality: A Conceptual Framework." *Implicit Religion* 12, no. 1 (April 1, 2009): 51–72.

Kwilecki, Susan. "Twenty-First-Century American Ghost: The After-Death Communications—Therapy and Revelation from beyond the Grave." *Religion and American Culture* 19, no. 1 (December 1, 2009): 101–33.

Lee, Philip J. *Against the Protestant Gnostics.* New York: Oxford University Press, 1987.

Lewis, Frank B. "Bible and Modern Religions: Modern Spiritualism." *Interpretation* 11, no. 4 (October 1, 1957): 438–54.

Lochhaas, Philip H. *The New Age Movement.* How to Respond to World Religions. St. Louis: Concordia, 1995.

Ludwig, David J., and Mary R. Jacob. *Christian Concepts for Care: Understanding and Helping People with Mental Health Issues.* St. Louis: Concordia, 2014.

Luther, Martin. *What Luther Says: A Practical In-Home Anthology for the Active Christian.* Compiled by Ewald M. Plass. St. Louis: Concordia, 1986.

Mazur, Eric Michael, and Kate McCarthy. "Part 3: Popular Spirituality and Morality" in *God in the Details: American*

Religion in Popular Culture. New York: Routledge, 2001.

McCain, Paul, et al., ed. *Concordia: The Lutheran Confessions.* St. Louis: Concordia, 2006.

McClendon, Adam. "Defining the Role of the Bible in Spirituality: 'Three Degrees of Spirituality' in American Culture." *Journal of Spiritual Formation and Soul Care* 5, no. 2 (September 2012): 207–25.

Mercado, Leonardo. "Christian and Interfaith Spirituality." *Dialogue and Alliance* 20, no. 2 (September 1, 2006): 17–31.

Musk, Bill. *The Unseen Face of Islam: Sharing the Gospel with Ordinary Muslims at Street Level.* Grand Rapids, MI: Monarch Books, 2004.

Naegeli-Osjord, Hans. *Possession & Exorcism.* Oregon, WI: New Frontiers Center, 1988.

Nartonis, David K. "The Rise of 19th-Century American Spiritualism, 1854–1873." *Journal for the Scientific Study of Religion* 49, no. 2 (June 1, 2010): 361–73.

Pew Research Center. "Eastern, New Age Beliefs Widespread: Many Americans Mix Multiple Faiths," www.pewforum.org/files/2009/12/multiplefaiths.pdf (accessed March 4, 2015).

Pool, Jeff B. "Toward Spirituality of Post-Christian Disciples of Jesus." *Communio Viatorum* 53, no. 1 (2011): 3–46.

Primiano, Leonard N. "Oprah, Phil, Geraldo, Barbara, and Things That Go Bump in the Night" in *God in the Details: American Religion in Popular Culture.* New York: Routledge, 2001.

Rosik, Christopher H. "When Discernment Fails: The Case for Outcome Studies on Exorcism." *Journal of Psychology and Theology* 25, no. 3 (1997): 356.

"Schizophrenia Spectrum and Other Psychotic Disorders" in *Diagnostic and Statistical Manual of Mental Disorders: DSM-5.*

Washington DC: American Psychiatric Association, 2013.

Schmidt, Leigh Eric. *Restless Souls: The Making of American Spirituality.* San Francisco: HarperSanFrancisco, 2005.

Schulz, Klaus Detlev. *Mission from the Cross: The Lutheran Theology of Mission.* St. Louis: Concordia, 2009.

Scott, Beverly. "Inner Spiritual Voices or Auditory Hallucinations." *Journal of Religion and Health* 36, no. 1 (March 1997): 53–63.

Sire, James W. *The Universe Next Door: A Basic Worldview Catalog.* Downers Grove, IL: InterVarsity Press, 2004.

Spinks, Bryan D. *Reformation and Modern Rituals and Theologies of Baptism: From Luther to Contemporary Practices.* Aldershot, England: Ashgate, 2006.

Stafford, Betty. "The Growing Evidence for 'Demonic Possession': What Should Psychiatry's Response Be?" *Journal of Religion and Health* 44, no. 1 (Spring 2005): 13–30.

Streib, Heinz, and Ralph W. Hood. "'Spirituality' as Private Experience-Oriented Religion: Empirical and Conceptual Perspectives." *Implicit Religion* 14, no. 4 (2011): 433–53.

Thompson, Marianne Meyer. *The Incarnate Word: Perspectives on Jesus in the Fourth Gospel.* Peabody, MA: Hendrickson Publishers, 1993.

Versteeg, Peter, and Johan Roeland. "Contemporary Spirituality and the Making of Religious Experience: Studying the Social in an Individualized Religiosity." *Fieldwork in Religion* 6, no. 2 (2012): 120–46.

Weller, Philip T., trans. *The Roman Ritual,* Complete Edition. Milwaukee: Bruce Publishing, 1964.

SCRIPTURE INDEX

SUBJECT INDEX

90, 92, 100, 113, 120, 123, 131, 135, 141, 169, 175; for idols/the dead, 44, 47, 53 (*see also* offerings [to idols/ spirits])

God's Word, 17, 31, 50, 68, 71, 72, 82, 90, 100, 116, 118, 120, 121, 123, 129, 130, 135, 137, 140, 142, 154, 166, 173–75

Gospel, 25, 71, 81, 98, 100, 117, 134, 139, 142, 145, 155

Haiti, 19, 21, 41, 43, 45, 128n

hallucination, 128, 162

healing, 43, 54, 78, 86, 88, 89, 98, 99, 120, 131

humanity, 10, 18, 30, 58, 60, 61, 62, 64, 66–67, 73, 74, 91, 115, 120, 122, 130, 162, 173, 174

human spirits, 21

hymn, 23, 29–36, 118–19, 136, 139–40

hypnotism, 98, 152–53

idolatry, 28–29, 44, 46–49, 148, 166, 167

incantation, 21, 28, 29

incarnation, 62, 65

justification, 72; doctrine of, 175

kingdom: of God, 9, 34, 36, 139; of the evil one, 9, 139

Laveau, Marie, 40–41, 50, 53, 54

liturgy, 12, 127, 132–41, 165, 174

Lord's Prayer, 28, 35, 118, 119, 138, 139, 147, 148

Lord's Supper, 12, 13, 14, 62, 90, 120, 149, 155, 166, 174. *See also* Sacraments

Lutheran Church, 14, 23, 26, 71, 105, 116, 131, 136

Luther, Martin, 12, 24, 25, 28, 35, 36, 100, 118–19, 123, 129–32, 133, 135, 138–40, 161, 164–66, 167, 168–69

Madagascar, 54, 56, 136, 138

magic, 28–29, 91, 99, 116, 119, 148, 162, 167, 170,

Marie Laveau. *See* Laveau, Marie

Martin Luther. *See* Luther, Martin

Means of Grace, 62, 175. *See also* Absolution; Baptism; God's Word; Lord's Supper

medium(s), 68, 97, 98–99, 154

mental health, 86, 90, 91, 107, 128, 129, 131, 140, 146, 147, 149, 150–53, 157, 161, 163, 168

mermaid, 43, 46–47

moralism, 6, 71

mysticism, 6, 62, 91, 98, 104, 142

naturalism, 6, 18, 56, 59, 63–65, 67, 68, 74, 78

necromancy, 6, 52, 67, 74, 81

New Orleans, 39, 40, 44, 54, 55

night terrors, 11, 23, 27, 28, 30, 121–22

nihilism, 6, 64–65

occult, 17–18, 40, 50, 91, 129, 133, 154, 162, 163

offerings (to idols/spirits), 21, 44, 46–47, 49, 50, 82

old Adam, 60, 122–23, 154. *See also* original sin

original sin, 35, 64, 122. *See also* old Adam

paganism, 49, 61, 69, 81, 82

paranormal, 6, 28, 68, 104, 106, 119

paranormal investigator, 6, 68, 119

peace, 27, 32, 36, 74, 107, 117, 120, 135, 138, 140, 156, 169, 174

Pentecostalism, 162

philosophy, 56, 59, 64, 67, 73, 79

possession, demon, 87, 105, 121, 127, 129–32, 140, 146, 150, 151, 153–54, 162, 163, 167, 173

postmodernism. *See* worldview: postmodern

prayer, 14, 28, 29, 32, 107, 116, 118, 119, 121, 127, 128, 130, 131, 134, 137, 138, 139, 148–49, 165–66, 174–75. *See also* Lord's Prayer

preaching, 11, 12, 62, 72, 90, 100, 117, 119, 137, 169, 173, 175. *See also* prosperity preaching; sermon pride, 24, 88, 140, 168, 170

priest: Roman Catholic, 45, 104, 106, 153, 163; voodoo, 19–22, 25–27, 41–45, 48, 54, 128n, 154, 167

prince of this world. *See* Satan

promise (of God), 13–15, 24, 25, 26, 27, 28, 31, 33, 35, 36, 71, 72, 74, 81, 90–92, 116, 120, 130, 134, 135, 137, 139, 141, 142, 145, 148, 149, 157, 166, 174–75

prosperity preaching, 19, 25

protection, 12–15, 23, 28, 29, 31, 34, 35, 116, 120, 121, 123, 128n, 130, 134, 141, 146

psychic, 98. *See also* medium(s)

Rationalism, 6, 63, 74, 105, 118, 140

reconciliation, 32, 62, 156

repentance, 24, 26. *See also* Confession

resurrection, 9, 13, 25, 28, 36, 52, 55, 65, 66, 74, 81, 90, 115, 116, 117, 135, 142, 145, 148, 155, 169, 170, 174, 175

righteousness, 24, 115, 167, 175

rite: of a house blessing, 116, 118, 167; of Baptism, 62, 164–66; of Confession and Absolution, 26, 62, 120, 134; of exorcism, 136, 138, 167; of the Church, 62, 71; voodoo, 41, 167

Roman Catholic Church, 26, 41, 105, 154, 164. *See also* priest: Roman Catholic

Sacrament of the Altar. *See* Lord's Supper

Sacraments, 12–13, 71, 90, 100, 119, 120, 123, 129, 130, 140–41, 169, 173–75. *See also* Absolution; Baptism; Lord's Supper

sacrifice: of Jesus, 10, 81; pagan, 21, 27, 49, 82

saints, 30, 32, 41, 103, 157, 175

salt, 43, 164–67

Satan, 9, 12–14, 18, 19, 24–36, 48, 49, 67, 70, 73, 88–89, 91, 95, 100, 105, 108, 115, 116, 118–19, 122–23, 130–32, 136, 138–40, 145, 156–57, 161, 166, 168–70, 174–75

schizophrenia, 128, 129. *See also* mental health

sermon, 33, 136, 138, 152. *See also* preaching

shaman, 78–81

siren. *See* mermaid

soul competency, doctrine of, 70

Southern Baptist Church, 70

spell, 21, 28, 29, 41, 42, 44, 116, 148, 162

spirituality, American, 11, 18, 35, 42, 43, 48, 49, 50, 56, 59, 63, 67, 69, 72–74, 81, 104

spiritual warfare, 11, 12, 14, 18, 22, 28, 30–31, 32, 35, 36, 68, 86, 91, 115, 122–23, 128, 138, 141, 146, 157, 161, 163, 168, 170, 173, 175

SSRIs (selective serotonin reuptake inhibitors), 129

suicide, 34, 64, 112, 131–32, 146, 149, 150

supernatural, 6, 18, 28

talisman, 28, 29

temple: voodoo, 43, 44–48; holy, 166

tomb, 52–56; of Jesus, 65, 174, 175

trance, 79, 86, 113

truth, 10, 14, 17, 27, 50, 67, 70, 72, 148, 175

unbelief, 11, 81, 123, 128n, 131, 167

utopia, 64

victory, 31, 32, 36, 123, 170, 175

video gaming, 85–91

vocation, 88, 89–92, 117, 147, 168

voodoo, 28, 29, 40–42, 50–51, 128. *See also* temple: voodoo; priest: voodoo; rite: voodoo

warning, 34, 49, 50, 81–82, 138, 141

warrior. *See* angels, holy

water, holy. *See* Baptism

worldview, 6, 59–60, 74; animistic/spiritual (*see* animism); biblical, 65–67, 68, 78, 140; naturalistic (*see* naturalism); postmodern, 59, 65, 67–69

Answers to the Study Questions

Chapter 1 Study Questions

1. How does Confession and Absolution come into play in the midst of spiritual warfare? Explain your answer using examples from the chapter.

Satan and his demons are effective at exposing and exploiting the sin that clings to us. Confession and Absolution therefore removes one of Satan's greatest weapons from his arsenal. To speak of one's sin openly to the pastor removes the hidden nature of sin. It removes the inner voice that seeks to justify oneself or drives oneself to despair with the fear of the sin becoming known. Moreover, the absolution of sins brings comfort to the sinner, because the sin that once plagued the conscience is removed by the Lord. Yet, the gift of absolution does not only remove the burden of a heavy conscience, it also declares a reality: the sin that clung to the individual is taken away by Jesus' command. It no longer exists; therefore, it cannot legitimately be used to intimidate a Christian.

2. What role can proper catechesis play in the midst of spiritual warfare? Explain your answer using examples from the chapter.

Christians who come from confessional traditions are used to hearing the word *catechesis*. They study their catechisms and learn the details of their faith. When it comes to spiritual warfare, catechesis becomes one of the most important weapons in the Christian's arsenal. The devil is the father of lies. His use of "The Lie" is one of his greatest weapons. Jesus has defeated the devil through His death and resurrection. The Christian already has freedom from the devil, but the devil is good at convincing his prey otherwise. Anyone facing spiritual attack must recognize who they are in view of Jesus. While it is true that sin still clings to the Christian, it is also true that God no longer views these sins as necessary for judgment. The world has already been judged in Jesus, and those who have received Jesus' holy name through Baptism have been transformed from the kingdom of darkness and have been brought into the kingdom of light. Nevertheless, if Satan and his demons can convince the

Christian that they still reside in the power of the devil, he has already won. Therefore, a Christian must understand that while the devil and his demons may still cause great physical and mental harm to them, he cannot change the fact that they are owned by Jesus. Once a Christian comes to this knowledge, the assaults of Satan lose their sting. The Christian trusts that Jesus is with him as He has promised to be (Matthew 28:20) and that he need no longer fall prey to the devil's propaganda.

So, what of non-Christians? Where can they go for help? The answer is the same for the Christian as it is for the non-Christian. Jesus has paid the price for all sin including the sin of the nonbeliever. Catechesis teaches the Gospel. The Gospel is the Good News for the world. When the Word of Jesus is proclaimed, it has the power to change the heart and mind. The Word of Jesus has the power to bring life to those who were born dead. Nonbelievers who are assaulted by the devil and his demons can find comfort in Jesus' crucifixion and resurrection because they, too, were included in Jesus' sacrifice. Jesus became sin so that He might release the burden of sin for all people.

3.   What example does Martin Luther provide when dealing with demonic assault?

The example provided in this chapter demonstrates how Martin Luther fought off spiritual attacks. First, Luther never attempted to justify his own sin. Instead, he recognized the burden of his own sin and his ongoing failures. When Satan came to Luther to accuse him and torment him over his sin, Luther did not argue or defend his actions. In fact, he accepted the truth of Satan's accusations. Second, in times of deep spiritual battle, Luther focused on Jesus. All of what the devil spoke was true, but it was covered in a lie. Jesus has removed the guilt of sin, and the Christian stands free. How could Luther be so sure of this? Luther's assurance was found outside of his own actions and upon the actions of another—namely, Jesus. He knew that Jesus' death was far greater than his own sinful condition and because of Jesus he was a new creation, one that is perfect just as Jesus is perfect.

4. **What does "prosperity preaching" teach? How did the prosperity preaching that Jill encountered help lead her into the spiritual darkness she endured?**

Prosperity preaching focuses on what an individual can receive if he or she is faithful enough to God. Most of the popular TV preachers are included in this category. You can usually recognize them by their expensive suits, mansions, and airplanes. They tell their viewers that God has blessed them because of their faithfulness. Their encouragement is clear: if you are faithful in your tithes, morality, and church attendance, you, too, will receive similar blessings. Moreover, the reverse is also clear: if you do not have such wealth and health, you must question your faith.

Jill was driven to despair by hearing such preaching. She questioned why she had not received the wealth she thought she had been promised by God. One who is in despair is willing to do almost anything to relieve that despair. Some people use drugs and alcohol, and others commit suicide. Jill chose yet a different option: she looked for a spiritual cure apart from Jesus. Satan is always ready to fill the gap of faith, and in this case he did so through the spiritual work of a voodoo priest. Jill unknowingly sought out the help of the devil for worldly gain rather than Jesus for eternal gain. The devil comes to us in various ways, yet at the same time his ways are not really that diverse. The devil comes in the ways we desire; that is, he comes with the lie of fulfilling our desires. He will be anyone we want him to be or provide any emotion we wish to experience. As the result of sin, we desire the miraculous, the spiritual, the mystical—but too often these things are only coverings for the evil one's activities. The only hope for us is Jesus. Nevertheless, Jesus does not come in overtly miraculous, spiritual, or mystical ways. Jesus comes in His Word proclaimed by sinners. Jesus comes in the midst of the water and Word in Holy Baptism. Jesus promises to be in the midst of His people through the gift of His body and blood in the Lord's Supper. Through these hidden things, we have a connection with the Creator of all things. Through the Word and the Sacraments, heaven and earth are connected through the presence of Jesus. Everything necessary for today and eternity resides before the Christian.

5. **Describe Jill's view of prayer. How could this view of prayer be problematic?**

Jill understood prayer in terms of incantation. She thought that she could use prayer as a magical spell or formula. This is how the pagan world understands prayer. Because of the sin that dwells within humanity, we are always looking for a way to control our own destiny. In essence, we want to be our own gods. We want the hidden power that allows us to control not only our physical world but also the heavenly and spiritual realms. For the Christian, prayer is not a magical formula but the God-given ability to speak to our Father in heaven. When we pray for spiritual protection, we are not casting a spell of protection but asking our heavenly Father to protect us as a faithful father protects his children. The Lord's Prayer is one of the most helpful prayers for one who is under spiritual attack. Yet, the power of this prayer is not in the words spoken by the one who prays them but in the power of the One who originally spoke them. The Lord's Prayer is a special prayer in two ways. First, it is the Word of God, the Word spoken by Jesus and given to the Church. This prayer carries with it the promise of Jesus' presence and the Father's promise of hearing the prayers of those who, through Holy Baptism, are now charged with calling Him Father. Second, this prayer is an exorcistic prayer that speaks the promise of God to deliver us from the evil one.

6. **How can the promise of Holy Baptism help us with the spiritual battles we face?**

Baptism identifies us as a child of God with the promise of protection and ultimate deliverance from sin, death, and the devil.

7. **How can Christian hymns provide assistance to those who are spiritually oppressed or possessed?**

When someone is under intense spiritual attack, it is difficult to think with a clear mind. Just ask anyone who has experienced intense depression. The mind becomes so filled with irrational thoughts that reality itself can be lost. Spiritual attack is similar to that which is experienced in depression. Spiritual attacks can take away the ability to think and even speak. Many times, one under spiritual attack is in such a state of spiritual bondage that he cannot bring himself to pray. The internal state is one of noise and fear. Such a person needs to hear a word from the outside. An external word is necessary to break through this rampart of darkness and death. This is where good, faithful Christian hymns provide rescue for those suffering in spiritual darkness.

Traditional Christian hymns are nothing other than the words of Scripture. They serve as the delivery means for the Word of God. They speak with an outside voice to the inward man. Moreover, the voice that is spoken is the voice of Jesus. He is the One who "breaks the darkness" (*LSB* 849) and stills the fear of His "little flock" (*LSB* 735). When the words of Jesus are spoken, Satan is defeated.

8. Review the list of hymns provided in the appendix. How can these hymns be described as exorcistic in nature?

Answers will vary depending on which hymn is examined. For an example of the exorcistic nature of these hymns, review the author's examination of the hymns provided in chapter 1.

9. Are you aware of any exorcistic hymns that are not included in the appendix but that might be helpful to one who is spiritually oppressed or possessed? If so, what are they, and where can they be found?

Answers will vary, but the focus of this question should be on those hymns or stanzas that speak specifically to the defeat of Satan and the promise of Jesus' presence in the midst of His people through His Word and Sacraments.

10. Describe the problems of attempting to engage in a spiritual battle by oneself.

As individuals, we are powerless against the attacks of the devil. Christian piety, faith, and knowledge are desirable spiritual traits that Christians should aspire to in their daily lives, but they are of little value in spiritual battles. Indeed, such things can even be used against a faithful Christian. How can this be? Fasting, prayer, and Christian piety are expressions of the eternal faith Christians have received by the grace of Jesus. Still, because of sin, these good and faithful practices can turn one's spiritual focus from the Savior to one's own personal piety. Satan and his demons are masterful at exploiting the personal piety of God's people. The only righteousness that counts when a Christian is attacked is what is called the alien righteousness of Jesus. The only righteousness any Christian possesses is a righteousness that is external to himself, specifically the righteousness of Jesus. St. Paul helps explain this alien righteousness when he uses the image of Christians being clothed in Christ Jesus through Holy Baptism (Galatians 3:27). Throughout the Scriptures, we are told of those who are gathered before the Lord wearing white robes (Revelation 6:11; 7:9). The white robes symbolize a covering that is pure and without sin, which covers the sins of those who are before the throne of the Lord. This is the righteousness that covers the baptized. Although, too often Christians begin to look to their own righteousness rather than the righteousness of Jesus. The problem with such misdirection is the fallacy of our own righteousness. Scripture is clear: no one is righteous apart from Jesus (Romans 3:10).

If Satan and his demons can trick the Christian into engaging with them personally, they have successfully removed Jesus from the conversation and replaced Him with the vulnerability of the individual. The Christian who faces spiritual attack must not engage Satan and his demons in direct battle. Jesus is the only exorcist. He is the only one who has power over the evil attackers. To talk about spiritual warfare or defense, apart from the presence of Jesus, is a fallacy that in the end brings only spiritual defeat. This is why it is necessary to understand how Jesus promises to be present in the life of the Christian. Where Jesus' Word is proclaimed and His Sacraments are properly administered, there is Jesus. Moreover, where Jesus is, Satan and his demons stand in the weakness of the judgment of the cross (John 12:31–37). The defense of the Christian is always external—that is, in the external Word and Sacraments in which Jesus has promised to be for the Christian.

Chapter 2 Study Questions

1. **Consider the story at the beginning of the chapter about a man and his son. Did this story surprise you? Why or why not? Explain your answers.**

Answers will vary depending on personal experience. Many readers may have grown up in a scientific and Rationalistic culture that denies spiritual entities and the miraculous. Therefore, too often they fail to identify the dangers of the occult and spiritualism. The man who took his son to the voodoo store seems to fit into this category.

2. **What was the biblical basis for the voodoo priest's protection spell as explained in the chapter? Why is such a use of Holy Scripture inconsistent with the Christian faith?**

The occult constantly misquotes and misuses Holy Scripture. The origin of this deception is found in the temptation narrative of Jesus (Matthew 4:1–11; Luke 4:1–13), where the devil seeks to mislead Jesus by a false representation of God's Word. In chapter 2, the voodoo priest used the words of Psalm 23 and the imagery of water. Using Scripture in such a way removes the emphasis from the promise of Jesus' presence and turns it into occult magic. The psalms are the voice of Jesus, but when used as magical incantations they are disconnected from His promise and are turned into a voice of lies.

3. **The voodoo temple described in the chapter included many Christian symbols intermixed with the symbols of other religions. Why are so many people drawn to such forms of pan-spirituality?**

Paul writes about this in 2 Timothy 4:1–5. In these verses, Paul describes the direction of false preachers. They seek to lead people away to myths or, in other words, to the lies of Satan (see John 8:44). People see the mystical, but in their search they fall prey to Satan and his demons. Many Christians are falling away from the Church these days. They are leaving the comfort of the liturgy in search of what they think is a more meaningful form of worship. The occult claims to bring people to a fuller understanding of the hidden powers of the world, and this causes many to question the reality of what is promised in the liturgy and seek a mystical experience. Such a desire can lead people into the occult without recognizing the dangers of their journey until they become lost in the spiritual darkness that is always found at the end of such journeys.

While the journey of the Divine Service may seem less exciting to the uninformed, at the heart of the liturgy is the presence of Jesus. The Divine Service is nothing other than the Word of Jesus. The liturgy of the Church finds its origins in Holy Scripture. The liturgy is the voice of Jesus for the benefit of His people. Yet, without the eyes of faith, the liturgy can seem to be uninspiring and uneventful. Nevertheless, although the Divine Service may seem simple, in it life is given, sin is removed, and the devil is cast away. Such things do not depend on the charisma of the pastor, the inspiring nature of the experience, or the aesthetics of the worship space; they depend only on the presence of Jesus.

4. **Read 2 Timothy 4. How does St. Paul's warning to Timothy apply to the content of this chapter?**

Answers to this question will vary, but the Christian must always use the Word of God as the measure of all experience, knowledge, and worship. Experiential stimuli cannot be trusted and many times can lead to spiritual danger. St. Paul's point is that such false theology is dangerous because we want it to be true so much that we will close our ears to the truth of Scripture and follow the lies of the devil.

5. **Have you ever left flowers or other items at the grave of a loved one? If so, what is the difference between the practices described in this chapter and that which you do for those who have departed?**

The point of this question comes down to motivation. Do you make use of such practices in an effort to communicate with the dead? Are you trying to provide gifts and resources for the one who is buried in the grave? Are you performing such acts out of duty to your parents, spouse, or children? If you answered "Yes" to any of the above, you have begun to journey into animism.

Such motivations are in conflict with the promise of the resurrection. Modern-day spiritualism has infected many areas of life and death. This lie claims that there is no hell or heaven but instead another plane of existence that continues to communicate with the living. Such belief is contrary to the biblical witness and has no place in the Christian mind. But if you visit the grave with the expectation of the resurrection and out of a deep caring for the bodily remains that will be reunited with the soul on the Last Day, such activities are godly and precious in the sight of the Lord.

6. **What does the term *necromancy* mean? Read Leviticus 19:31; 20:6; 20:27; Deuteronomy 18:9–12; 1 John 4:1; Isaiah 8:19; 1 Timothy 4:1; and 2 Corinthians 11:14. How does God view necromancers?**

Necromancy is the desire to communicate with the dead. Such activity is destructive to the truth of God and leads to the work of the devil. People who claim to speak to the dead cause great harm to themselves and their hearers. God condemns such behavior and attaches to His condemnation severe consequences.

Chapter 3 Study Questions

1. **Describe the three most popular worldviews found within American society.**

Although there are various worldviews in a country as vast as the United States, the three most popular worldviews are naturalism, spiritualism, and Christianity. Naturalism views the world as a closed system without the possibility of miracles. Spiritualism takes the direct opposite view of the world and sees it as an open system filled with various spiritual entities that can interact with humanity. Spiritualists expect and encourage miracles. Spiritualism can also be known under the terms *mysticism* and *animism*. The third worldview, which remains common within the United Sates, is what is referred to in this book as the biblical worldview. The biblical worldview uses the revealed Word of God as the lens through which it views the world. While the other two worldviews are at odds with a biblical worldview, the biblical worldview can accept various elements of the others. For instance, the biblical worldview accepts the demonstrational aspects of the sciences found in naturalism. Moreover, the biblical worldview is based on the reality of miracles and the spiritual realities of life after death. While the biblical worldview is often accused of being closed-minded and unwilling to accept the worldview of others, it is actually the more inclusive of the three worldviews. However, although the biblical worldview is open to some of the tenets of the other worldviews, it limits its openness to those things that are in line with the Holy Bible.

2. What do you think is at the heart of the fears most people face?

Doubt always brings with it fear. The world is a dangerous place, and at the end of everyone's life is the problem of death. Only the biblical worldview provides hopeful answers to these problems. While naturalism's end is nothingness, spiritualism's end is filled with unanswered questions. The Bible begins with the problem that is common to all humanity: sin and its end, which is death. However, unlike the other two worldviews, the Bible describes the redemptive plan of the Creator, which comes through the incarnation, Baptism, ministry, death, and resurrection of Jesus the Christ.

3. In your own words, how would you describe animism? What aspects of animism have you noticed around you this week?

Answers to this question will vary based on each person's background and experience.

4. Describe objective justification. How does the doctrine of objective justification differ from subjective justification?

Objective justification is the doctrine that describes how God has declared the entire world righteous, including all people of the past and present, through the incarnation, Baptism, obedience, crucifixion, and resurrection of Jesus. While the doctrine of objective justification includes all humanity, the doctrine of subjective justification is person specific. Subjective justification focuses on Christ's redemption work—His work of salvation centered in the cross—and delivers it to the individual sinner. The delivery mechanisms of this justification are the Word and the Sacraments of Baptism and the Lord's Supper. Through these Means of Grace, Jesus brings the gift of salvation, life, and freedom to those who were born dead and under the influence of the devil (see Ephesians 2).

5. In view of what you have read in this chapter, how do you view the topic of ghosts? Has this chapter changed your mind? Why or why not?

Answers to this question will vary based on each person's background and experience.

6. Does 1 Samuel 28:7–19 prove the existence of ghosts?

The identity of the spirit represented in the text remains under debate. Was it the prophet who spoke to King Saul, or was it a demonic spirit? The text reports the spirit to be the prophet. Still, Christians must be cautious about establishing a doctrine of ghosts based on one text. Moreover, the topic of necromancy or communicating with the dead is severely condemned in the Bible. Some might suggest that if the Bible warns its readers not to seek out communications with the dead, then there must be the possibility of such communications. Nevertheless, such conclusions are flawed in light of the rest of Scripture. Scripture warns Christians that the devil and his demons can successfully impersonate the holy angels. What would prevent such lying spirits from impersonating the dead?

7. Why would a naturalist deny the possibility of miracles?

Those who hold to a naturalistic worldview look to so-called natural causes for the unknown things of the world. For the naturalist, all things would require an evolutionary development. Life and death are natural events tied to a cause-and-effect relationship. For the naturalist, there is only the cosmos. Naturalism understands the cosmos to be a "closed system"—that is, a system without spiritual influences.

8. **What does it mean to describe one's faith as "spiritual but not religious"? Is such a view of faith compatible with the Christian faith demonstrated in the pages of Holy Scripture? Explain your answer.**

Those who describe themselves as "spiritual but not religious" lack a trust in organizations and institutions. They have disconnected their spirituality from religion in the formal sense and find their ultimate meaning in their own experiences apart from the dogmas of organized religion. This individualistic spirituality claims to provide for a personal relationship with the divine. Such a faith is incompatible with the Christian faith, which focuses on a worshiping community gathered around the pure preaching/teaching of the Word and the right administration of the Sacraments (see Article 7 of the Augsburg Confession).

9. **What is the doctrine of soul competency? What difficulties does this chapter find with such a doctrine?**

The doctrine of soul competency requires that individualistic precedence is placed over creedal acceptance. When taken to its logical conclusions, this doctrine destroys the possibility of confessional subscription and allows for various interpretations to exist side by side within the Church. The problems such an inconsistent theology can bring to those within the Church who have minimal biblical knowledge should be evident: inconsistency leads to anxiety during times of personal struggles, and anxiety leads to fear.

10. **One of the reasons people give for leaving the Church is the oppressive nature they find in the dogmas of the Church. Do you agree or disagree with their concerns? Explain your answer.**

We live in a society that denies objective truth and seeks to replace dogma with personal experience. The Word of God presents itself as a divine revelation of truth (John 17:17–19) that is "profitable for teaching, for reproof, for correction, and for training in righteousness, that the man of God may be complete, equipped for every good work" (2 Timothy 3:16–17). Therefore, the teachings of the Bible contain corrective measures, which are called divine Law, such as the Ten Commandments. The preaching of the Law will always create rebellion within the sinful condition that seeks its own desires. However, the Law is the alien work of God meant to show sinners their helpless condition. This helplessness then opens the way to the hearing of the Gospel message of Christ crucified for the forgiveness of sins. Therefore, it is necessary to bend one's will to the Word of God and trust in His promises.

Chapter 4 Study Questions

1. **What is your view of American Indian culture? Is it compatible with Christianity? Explain your answer.**

Answers to the first question will vary based on each person's background and experience. However, because American Indian culture is connected with spiritualism, it would be difficult to incorporate it into Christianity without the problem of syncretism (the fixing of different religions).

2. **Have you ever participated in an American Indian ceremony like the one described in this chapter? If so, how did your experience compare to the story in this chapter?**

Answers to this question will vary based on each person's background and experience.

3. **The story the Indian shaman taught his hearers claimed that all religions are connected to the same God. Is such a statement true? Explain your answer.**

The shaman's statement is true if we speak in terms of false religions. All of the false religions in the world have a common god—namely, Satan. In this sense, the shaman is correct. Nevertheless, there is only one true God and one true religion. This is the triune God—Father, Son, and Holy Spirit—who reveals Himself through Holy Scriptures. Our God is a jealous God who refuses to share His name with any false religion.

4. Now that you have read this chapter, what thoughts do you have about including various aspects of American Indian religious practices in the worship of the Church?

Answers to this question will vary based on each person's background and experience.

Chapter 5 Study Questions

1. How do some video games appeal to our common sinful condition?

Many of the video games offered these days provide an alternate sense of reality that leads people to live out fantasies that they would not consider in real life. Such games may encourage killing of police officers, theft, and sexual acts within the supposed safety of the alternative world of cyberspace. Sins of the mind are condemned by Jesus. One example is Jesus' understanding of adultery. Jesus teaches that the mental act of adultery is sinful even if it is not carried out in the flesh (Matthew 5:28; 15:19).

2. Is it acceptable for a Christian to play video games like the one described in the story? Explain your answer.

There is nothing inherently evil with video games. Indeed, they can serve as a God-pleasing form of entertainment as long as they are not misused. Still, there are many aspects of video games that appeal to the fallen nature. Therefore, Christians should avoid playing games that encourage sinful acts or lead to addictive behavior.

3. What are your thoughts about the man described in the story? Was he facing a spiritual problem as a result of his video game usage? If so, what was the nature of his problem, and how did it affect his faith?

The man's attachment to the video game was preventing him from fulfilling his vocation as a student and also interfering with his ability to care for his neighbors. Additionally, the excessive attachment to the game was becoming an alternate reality, thereby placing him into a dissociated state of consciousness. Christians are warned of the necessity of remaining "sober-minded and watchful" of the spiritual dangers that await them (1 Peter 5:8). Moreover, the excessive attachment to the video game affected him in a dangerous way. Because of his obsession, he had separated himself from the protective presence of Jesus, who delivers faith and salvation through the means of His Word and Sacraments.

4. **In the end, the man was freed from his video game addiction. How did the man regain his freedom?**

The man in the story overcame his addiction by entering a treatment facility and reconnecting himself to the Church. God establishes both of these institutions for the care of His people. The mental health professionals at the treatment facility were acting as a means of God's mercy, while the Church was acting as a means of His grace. The Christian is wise to attack the addictions in his life by using all the means that God provides. God serves His creation through the vocation of others. In the medical field, God serves through the vocations of doctors, nurses, and others who care for the needs of His people. In the Church, God serves through the Office of the Holy Ministry, which functions as the distribution point for His Means of Grace—namely, the Word and the Sacraments.

Chapter 6 Study Questions

1. **Have you ever attended a spiritual expo like the one mentioned in this chapter? If so, describe your experience. How did it compare to the events described above?**

Answers to this question will vary based on each person's background and experience.

2. **What, if any, dangers are there for Christians who attend an event like the one in this chapter?**

While Christians do not need to worry about their salvation being affected by attending such an event, they do face the possibility of falling prey to the lies that surround these types of events. The danger for Christians comes when they shift from being spectators to participants. The appeal of the occult is strong to sinful nature. Moreover, Christians who are tempted to visit such a place must ask themselves why they would desire to do so. If the answer to this question is examined in light of Scripture, there are few exceptions that would allow for such a visit, and curiosity is not a sufficient answer.

3. **Many unbelievers view Christians as hypocrites. Do you think this is a fair assumption? Explain your answer.**

Are Christians hypocrites? Yes, in one sense all Christians are hypocrites. All Christians claim moral standards yet fail to live up to these standards. The Ten Commandments are the standards to which all faithful Christians profess their adherence. Although no Christian can faithfully fulfill the demand of these commandments, all Christians can recognize in their failures the need for a Savior. Therefore, Christians carry sin into the Church so their sin may be washed away by Jesus, who promises His righteousness to the unrighteous.

4. **How many Americans have visited a medium or psychic in their lifetime? Does the answer surprise you? Why or why not?**

The statisticians quoted in the chapter report that 15 percent of Americans have sought the council of mediums, psychics, or fortune-tellers. The answers to the second part of this question will vary based on individual experience.

5. **What warning does Scripture give about seeking spiritual answers in places like the expo described above? (See Galatians 1:8–9.)**

When you look into the occult for answers, you will only find answers that appeal to your sinful nature. Sin desires to justify its own actions. Christians are not to look for the desires of their heart but to the promise found in the revealed Word of God.

Chapter 7 Study Questions

1. **According to the survey quoted in this chapter, what percentage of Americans report seeing a ghost or communicating with the dead? What are your thoughts about this statistic? Did the percentage seem high to you? Why or why not?**

The statistic in this chapter reported that 47 percent of Americans have communicated with the dead or believe in ghosts. Answers to the second question will vary depending upon personal experiences.

2. **Why did the Christian family in this story seek out the assistance of the paranormal investigators?**

The family in the story sought help from their church but received none. Their pastor had not been trained in how to deal with their problem and quite possibly did not believe their story. His only suggestion to them was to seek help from a Roman Catholic priest. Because their church was unable to provide an answer to the problem, they sought the help of a paranormal community.

3. **Do ghosts exist? What Scripture passages help answer this question?**

This book does not accept the possibility of ghosts that haunt the earth. The verses specifically mentioned in this chapter were Hebrews 9:27 and Philippians 1:23, however, participants may mention other biblical passages.

Chapter 8 Study Questions

1. Why do some pastors avoid the topic of exorcism?

Many pastors have not been trained in the area of spiritual warfare and exorcism. Therefore, they question their own worthiness and ability to face the devil and his demons. Still, as this book has made clear, the most important thing anyone can learn about exorcism is that its effectiveness has nothing to do with the pastor's training or worthiness. Proper pastoral training in spiritual warfare is focused on the work of Jesus. The only requirement placed upon the pastor is the requirement of faithfulness to the vows he has promised to uphold with the help of God.

2. Why did Pastor Smith seek the assistance of a brother pastor before assisting the family in the story?

The example of two pastors being sent out together to face the spiritual battles of the world finds its genesis in Jesus' ministry. In Luke 10:1–20, Jesus sends out the Seventy-Two to bring His message to the surrounding countryside. Moreover, the text specifically mentions that Jesus sent them out two by two. When the disciples returned, one of the things that they mentioned was their victories over the evil spirits. All wise pastors should recognize the need to get assistance from other experienced pastors.

3. What role did Baptism play in this story?

Baptism brings the promise of life from death. Scripture speaks about all people being born in a state of spiritual death (see Ephesians 2) before faith comes to them. Baptism has a transforming effect upon them. It transforms them from the power of the devil and the darkness of death into the kingdom of God (Colossians 1:13). In the case of the children in the story, Baptism served as an exorcism. While this exorcism was not of the sensational nature portrayed in Hollywood films, it was a true exorcism that Jesus performed through the lips and the hands of the pastor. Everyone who is baptized has received an exorcism.

4. Where might one find the connection between exorcism and the crucifixion in John's Gospel?

The clearest passage in Scripture that connects the crucifixion of Jesus to the exorcism of Satan is found in John 12:31–37. In this passage, Jesus promises that, through His crucifixion, the devil would be cast out (exorcized) from his place of power and control.

5. How are Baptism, exorcism, the crucifixion, and the resurrection of Jesus connected?

Romans 6 connects Baptism to the crucifixion and resurrection of Jesus. If the crucifixion was an exorcism of the devil, as John 12:31–37 states, then Baptism is connected to the exorcism of Satan.

6. What does the liturgical rite of a house blessing involve? Ask your pastor to review the rite with you.

Based on which agenda is used, the rites will differ. For a Lutheran pastor, the rite is found in the *Lutheran Service Book: Agenda*. Remember, these rites are not magical spells. They are words that the pastor speaks on behalf of Jesus as he performs the exorcism.

7. Read Matthew 12:43–45 and Luke 11:26. What do these verses teach us about demon possession and the activities of demons?

Just getting rid of a demon is not enough. These verses demonstrate that demons can return after an exorcism and cause greater harm than before they were cast out the first time.

Many people who are under spiritual attack seek a quick cure for their spiritual problems. But if the void of unbelief is not filled with the presence of Jesus and His gift of faith, such people will find additional suffering instead of relief. That is why it is important to remain connected to the Church and the gifts of Jesus' Word and Sacraments. These gifts bring Jesus into the life of the person and prevent Satan and his demons from slipping back into their seat of control.

8. **Is the personal holiness or piety of a person a factor in his or her ability to drive an evil spirit from a house? Explain your answer.**

The answer is no! While Christians should desire and even strive for personal piety, their piety has no sway on the activities of the devil. The example of Satan's outright attack on the holy Son of God (Matthew 4:1–11) should expel any hope that Christians might find in their own flawed piety. Jesus is the only one who has the power over the devil. Apart from the protection Christians have been granted in Jesus, they are like defenseless sheep before a hungry wolf.

9. **Why are Christian devotions an important part of the Christian life? Why are they especially important to the Christian who is facing a spiritual struggle like the one described in this chapter?**

Christian devotions are rooted in the words of Holy Scripture. Where Jesus' Word is proclaimed, Jesus has promised to be as our Savior from sin, death, and the devil. Devotions should be a part of every Christian's spiritual life, but this is especially true of one who is under direct spiritual attack. Where Jesus dwells, the devil and his demons will flee.

Chapter 9 Study Questions

1. **What brought on the spiritual attacks that Randy described?**

Randy sought to live in two different worlds. On Sunday mornings, he played the role as a church leader and organist for his church. Outside of the church service, he sought to control the hidden spiritual forces and use their power for his own purpose. As a result of his open sin, Satan stepped in to torment him until he finally persuaded the man to leave the church. Randy fell under the lie of Satan and believed himself to be outside of Jesus' love and forgiveness. Eventually, Randy gave in to the power of the devil and was afflicted by depression and anxiety, eventually leading to a complete mental breakdown.

2. **What is the evil eye? Should Christians worry about being cursed by others?**

Many occult religions believe that if someone looks at another person with evil intent the person receiving the gaze will fall under a curse. However, Christians need not worry about such a curse, because they carry the promise of Jesus. Such a promise does not mean that Christians will be free from the attacks of sin, death, and the devil. Still, Christians are promised that no matter what happens to them in life or death, they have the promise of life, forgiveness, and peace.

3. **Why did Randy's home pastor avoid helping him when he learned of the spiritual attacks the man was enduring?**

Randy's pastor had not received the proper training, and he had an unhealthy fear of the devil and his demons.

4. **How did the Rite of Confession and Absolution provide comfort and release to Randy?**

The Rite of Confession and Absolution erased the lies that Satan had used to bind Randy in fear and isolation. He had thought himself to be outside of the forgiveness of Jesus because of the magnitude of his sin. Yet, when Randy confessed his sins, the response he received was filled with words of the love of God and the promises of Jesus. Randy's sins were no longer before him because in the Words of Absolution they were replaced with the voice of life, peace, and forgiveness.

5. **How is Confession and Absolution connected to exorcism?**

Confession moves sins from the darkness of the heart and places them in the light of Jesus. Absolution declares God's promise and brings Jesus' presence to the one making the confession. The truth of Jesus always dislodges the lies of the devil. Whenever the devil and his demons are cast away, an exorcism has taken place.

6. Why did Randy find comfort in his Baptism?

Baptism is the visible Word. As sinners, we need more than just words. To be sure, God's Word is not just mere words like the everyday words we hear. God's Word has the power to create a reality when spoken. Many sinners question the Word of God. Therefore, God has provided the Word added to the water as a visible sign of His promise. While people might question what they hear, Baptism is an outward act with a physical element. Are they baptized? If the answer is yes, then God's promise is sure. Randy had forgotten this fact. He needed to be reminded what his Baptism meant. Once he heard these words, his comfort began to return because it was a comfort rooted in Jesus' promises.

7. What were the key elements of the short sermons preached during the exorcism?

Each of the sermons focused on the power of Jesus over the evil spirits. The first sermon focused on the promise that God is not a far-off God but one who promises to hear the pleas of His children. The second sermon focused on the salvific nature of Baptism. The final sermon demonstrated the authority that Jesus has granted to His pastors to forgive sins and thereby cast Satan and his demons away from God's people

8. What is it about the Lord's Prayer that is specifically exorcistic in nature?

The Seventh Petition of the Lord's Prayer is exorcistic in that it asks God to deliver His children from the evil one.

9. How were Christian hymns used in the exorcism?

Each of the hymns chosen for the exorcism were also miniature sermons specifically intended to comfort Randy and counterattack the devil and his demons. They were hymns of victory for the spiritually oppressed man, but they were hymns of torment for the devil.

10. What do you think about the phrase "exorcism as liturgy"? Is this a new way of understanding the church service on Sunday morning?

Answers to this question will vary based on each person's background and experience.

11. What relief, if any, did Randy receive from the exorcism?

Randy, who had hidden away in his small home for years, was now, at least in a limited way, back in his community. He was taking daily walks and playing Christian hymns on his home organ. Yes, he continued to have many problems. Apart from ongoing pastoral care, he faced the real possibility of his condition returning. Nevertheless, the exorcism provided relief, which was never obtained through psychiatry and pharmacology alone.

Chapter 10 Study Questions

1. Why is it necessary to remember that Jesus is the only exorcist?

Mankind, through its sinful nature, is in allegiance with Satan and his demons. While the new man of faith continues to fight against the old man of death, the Christian will not be totally freed from the sinful nature until death. Even though the devil is a defeated foe, he is still actively seeking to destroy the prize of God's creation—namely, humanity. Moreover, even in his weakened state the devil is far wiser and more powerful than any mortal man. Only Jesus has the authority or the power to vanquish the devil and his demons. Jesus is the only exorcist.

2. Can spiritual problems and mental problems always be differentiated? Explain your answer.

It is the assertion of this book that differentiating between mental problems and spiritually imposed problems is rarely possible. While certain symptoms can sometimes be recognized, the absence of these symptoms does not confirm or deny a demonic presence or oppression. Some of the outward symptoms that could demonstrate a demonic influence or possession are listed for reference.

The modern list includes physical, psychological, and spiritual indicators. They are included here for comparison.

Physical indicators:

1. The presence of a different voice—particularly one proclaiming fear or hatred

2. Convulsions in the individual when the evil spirit is exorcized

3. Occurrences of unwanted, forced behavior

4. Anesthesia to pain

5. Superhuman strength

6. Levitation

7. Poltergeist phenomena

Psychological indicators:

1. Appearances of a separate personality

2. Subjectively experiencing the entity as not being part of him/herself

3. Hearing an internal voice that does not have an associated personality

4. Experiencing confusion or clouding of consciousness

5. Sudden and complete relief experienced after exorcism

6. No benefit from therapy or medication

7. Addictive patterns of behavior

8. Telepathy or clairvoyance of other paranormal knowledge is present; for example, speaks fluently and/or understands a previously unknown language

Spiritual indicators:

1. Revulsion to the name of Jesus, Christian symbols, and/or prayer

2. Arrogant attitude

3. Stark change in moral character

4. Lack of spiritual growth in Christians

5. Prior occult involvement[42]

3. Doris had a deep affection for the Lord's Prayer. What was the problem identified in this chapter with her use of this most holy prayer?

Doris turned the Lord's Prayer into a magical incantation. This occurred when she disconnected the prayer from Jesus. Rather than praying the prayer as a child prays to her loving father, she began praying the prayer as if speaking magical words. She was looking to the prayer as a means of control and power. Unknowingly, Doris had removed the promise of Jesus and replaced Him with the way of the occult.

4. Review the exorcistic prayer provided in this chapter. What key points can you identify in this prayer?

Answers to this question will vary. The intention of the prayer was to call upon the name and protection of Jesus while at the same time ridiculing the devil.

5. Should pastors perform exorcisms on anyone who asks for them?

Although other faithful pastors may disagree on this issue, the author of this book answers in the negative.

6. Should a Christian avoid hypnotism? Why or why not? Explain your answer.

The practices of hypnotism are dangerous. First Peter 5:8–9 warns, "Be sober-minded; be watchful. Your adversary the devil prowls around like a roaring lion, seeking someone to devour. Resist him, firm in your faith." The danger of hypnotism lies in the attempt to dissociate the conscious and un-

---

42 Christopher H. Rosik, "When Discernment Fails: The Case for Outcome Studies on Exorcism," *Journal of Psychology and Theology* 25, no. 3 (1997): 356. See also Hans Naegeli-Osjord, *Possession & Exorcism* (Oregon, WI: New Frontiers Center, 1988), 176.

conscious mind, thereby removing the person's ability to assert his or her will. Hypnotism leaves the individual susceptible to outside suggestion, but Scripture warns that there are evil spiritual forces lying in wait for us and that we must not give our will over to another but remain aware of the spiritual danger that surrounds us.

7. **Can the words of a demon be trusted? What about those demons that are "bound" by the Word of God to speak the truth by the exorcist?**

Scripture is clear that the devil is the father of lies. Therefore, nothing he or his demons say should be considered trustworthy or true. Those who believe that they can "bind" the devil in such a way as to force him or his demons to speak the truth do so apart from the command of Scripture.

8. **Is it possible for a Christian to be under the power of a generational curse?**

A Christian is a child of God. Romans 8:31–39 is clear: nothing can separate the Christian from the love of God. Therefore, the possibility of a generational a curse is outside of the truths of God's revealed Word. However, as noted in the story, the devil can convince the children of God into believing such lies.

9. **What four questions does this chapter offer to help those who worry about being under a generational curse?**

If someone is concerned about the possibility of falling under a generational curse, the following questions can be used as a starting point:

- Are you baptized? If so, what does this mean about your relationship to God? (See Roman 6:3–4.)

- Do you trust in Jesus? What does His crucifixion do to the power of the devil? (See John 12:31.)

- Who is more powerful: Jesus? or Satan and his demons? (See Colossians 1:15–18.)

- In light of these passages and others, can Christians have a generational curse that places them into the control of Satan as his property?

10. What does Colossians 1:15–23 teach us about the authority of Jesus over the devil and his demons?

The first chapter of Colossians teaches that Jesus is the Creator of all things and that nothing in creation can exist without Him (v. 17). The things of creation include "thrones or dominions or rulers or authorities" (v. 16). In this passage, Paul is referring to the angelic world, which includes the holy angels and those who have fallen from glory. If such spiritual forces cannot exist or be held together without Jesus, it stands that Jesus has all authority over the devil and his demons.

Chapter 11 Study Questions

1. Why do people find it more desirable to seek answers from science rather than faith when dealing with the possibility of visual or audio hallucinations?

Science suggests that any problem can be answered if the right variables are understood. Because people are trained in the scientific method, they tend to engage spiritual exploration with Rationalist tools. Nevertheless, the problems of a spiritual nature cannot be easily quantified. Therefore, Western people tend to seek answers in ways that present the possibility of certainty over uncertainty.

2. What did the interim pastor do wrong according to this chapter?

The interim pastor relied on unbiblical methods in an attempt to control the devil.

3. What possible problems did Martin Luther find with the blessing of objects?

Although Luther did not find such an action to be heretical, he understood the potential for error that could result in blessing objects other than the divinely mandated Sacraments of Holy Baptism and the Lord's Supper.

4. **How are religious practices involving the use of holy water and other religious symbols problematic when used within the context of exorcism?**

The uses of such practices are not harmful in themselves. The problem with such practices is that they can be misunderstood by the uninformed. These rituals can also become idols when they are believed to carry a spiritual power.

5. **Should an exorcism ever take the place of medical attention? Explain your answer.**

Exorcism should never take the place of medical treatment. God works through means and vocations. Physicians and their medical expertise are God's means for the treatment and healing of physical and mental afflictions. To exclude God's means would be a misuse of God's gifts. Moreover, often a person who is possessed will be in need of medical care due to the injuries that result from his affliction and to receive hydration and nourishment. Such medical issues should always be considered in connection with an exorcism.[43]

6. **Should one use ridicule against the devil and his demons when engaged in a spiritual battle?**

Answers to this question will vary based on each person's background and experience. However, as a result of the crucifixion and resurrection, the Church is constantly ridiculing Satan through the act of preaching, teaching, absolving, and administering the Sacraments. These gifts not only bring eternal benefits to those who hear and receive them, but they also continue to mock the devil as one who has been cast out of his position of power. If we understand Luther's advice to ridicule the devil as one speaking in the stead of the Lord, his advice is well taken (see Jude 1:9).

---

43 In chapter 5 of *Christian Concepts for Care* (St. Louis: Concordia, 2014), Dr. David Ludwig focuses on the spiritual nature of mental and emotional disorders, showing how critical defining moments in a person's life can create a belief system that can drive the person's consciousness into anxiety, depression, and resentment: powerful forces that can have demonic effects on the person's life. This is a spiritual battle to define reality for the person: a battle between the old and new self. The Holy Spirit creates a new reality for the person, healing the damaged "spiritual DNA" that produced the emotional disorders.

7. **What does the chapter suggest to be the only foundation for success when one is involved in spiritual warfare?**

The only success found in spiritual warfare is the success that Jesus grants. Indeed, it is the only success that can be trusted. Satan is the father of lies, and he can easily turn a seeming victory into a defeat. Jesus is our Savior. In Jesus, the future of the Christian is sure. It is a future of life, resurrection, and eternity with God. Against the power of Jesus' name, the devil has no defense.